Patrick Butler

A BIOGRAPHY

HAZELDEN'S PIONEERS

Patrick Butler

A BIOGRAPHY

Damian McElrath, Ph.D.

WITH A FOREWORD BY GORDON GRIMM

50th
1949-1999
HAZELDEN

HAZELDEN
HP
PITTMAN
Archives
Press

HAZELDEN®
INFORMATION & EDUCATIONAL SERVICES

Hazelden
Center City, Minnesota 55012-0176
1-800-328-9000
1-651-257-1331 (Fax)
www.hazelden.org

Library of Congress Cataloging-in-Publication Data
McElrath, Damian.
     Biography of Patrick Butler / Damian McElrath.
          P.   CM. — (Hazelden's pioneers)
     Includes bibliographical references.
     ISBN 1-56838-309-6
     1. Butler, Patrick, 1900-1990. 2. Hazelden Foundation—Employees—
Biography. 3. Hazelden Foundation—History. 4. Alcoholism counselors—
Minnesota—Biography. 5. Alcoholics—Rehabilitation—Minnesota—History.
6. Substance abuse—Treatment—Minnesota—History. I. Title. II. Series.
     HV5281.H39M39   1998   98-35226
                                                                        CIP

03 02 01 00 99 5 4 3 2 1

Cover design by David Spohn
Interior design by Nora Koch / Gravel Pit Publications
Typesetting by Nora Koch / Gravel Pit Publications
Special thanks to editor Gretchen Bratvold

Contents

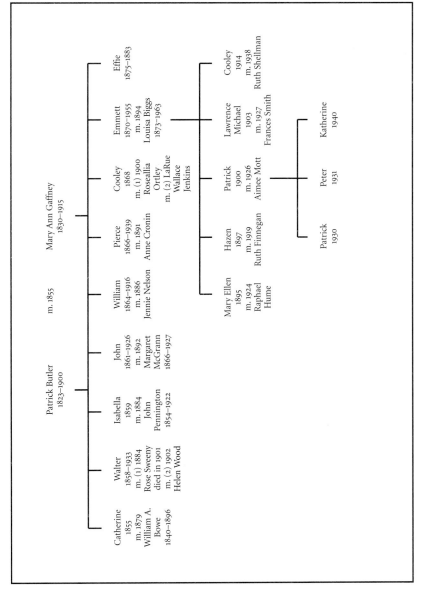

Butler Family Tree

Patrick Butler
1823–1900

m. 1855

Mary Ann Gaffney
1830–1915

Catherine
1855
m. 1879
William A.
Bowe
1840–1896

Walter
1858–1933
m. (1) 1884
Rose Sweeny
died in 1901
m. (2) 1902
Helen Wood

Isabella
1859
m. 1884
John
Pennington
1854–1922

John
1861–1926
m. 1892
Margaret
McGrann
1866–1927

William
1864–1916
m. 1886
Jennie Nelson

Pierce
1866–1939
m. 1891
Anne Cronin

Cooley
1868
m. (1) 1900
Roseallia
Ortley
m. (2) LaRue
Wallace
Jenkins

Emmett
1870–1955
m. 1894
Louisa Biggs
1873–1963

Effie
1875–1883

Mary Ellen
1895
m. 1924
Raphael
Hume

Hazen
1897
m. 1919
Ruth Finnegan

Patrick
1900
m. 1926
Aimee Mott

Lawrence
Michael
1903
m. 1927
Frances Smith

Cooley
1914
m. 1938
Ruth Shellman

Patrick
1930

Peter
1931

Katherine
1940

Gordon Grimm

Gordon Grimm began his career in 1960 at Willmar State Hospital in Willmar, Minnesota, where he worked as a chaplain assigned to the alcohol unit. In 1965, Grimm left Willmar to become Hazelden's first full-time pastor. Until his retirement in 1995, Grimm held a number of positions on both the clinical and training sides of the organization.

FOREWORD BY GORDON GRIMM

Patrick Butler's contributions to the field of alcohol and drug treatment were both unique and sweeping. Once in recovery himself, Pat poured his heart and soul into his efforts to raise public awareness about the nature of addiction and to develop effective treatment for the disease. And over time, Hazelden became the primary vehicle for the realization of his vision.

The breadth and success of Pat's contributions sprang in part from the life experiences he brought to Hazelden and the treatment field. His terms in the Ohio state legislature gave him an understanding of government and the legislative process. Both the Butler family and the family of his wife, Aimee Mott Butler, had long contributed to various charitable organizations; thus, Pat became familiar with the world of not-for-profit organizations.

Pat's background and experience with his father's business, particularly in the mining industry, made him a very successful businessman, and his business acumen helped Hazelden gain and maintain a solid financial foundation. Pat's family background and upbringing also gave him access to all levels of our society.

It was Pat's own recovery, however, that helped him recognize that at a basic level, all of us are the same, regardless of our economic or social standing. Pat also deeply appreciated the importance of family and the support it can provide as well as the role it can and must play in recovery from addiction.

Despite the knowledge and expertise he possessed, Pat was also what we'd call today a lifelong learner. Soon after he became sober,

"Underlying all of Pat's work was one goal: to help suffering alcoholics, and to do so with love and understanding."
—Gordon Grimm

Pat enrolled in the Yale Summer School of Alcohol Studies. He sought out and studied the research of the experts of the day, such individuals as Ray McCarthy and Selden Bacon of Yale University, John Pischuetti of the University of Montana, and Mark Keller, who became the editor of the *Journal on Alcohol Studies*. Pat also made a point of working with other treatment leaders such as Pat Cronin, founder of Pioneer House, and Nelson Bradley, then director of Willmar State Hospital. Throughout his life, Pat stayed abreast of the field's latest developments.

Recognizing, too, that a single treatment center, no matter how good, couldn't be everything to everybody, Pat did what he could to support other work in the field. The impetus and funding for the University of Minnesota's first counseling course with a focus on alcoholism came from Pat Butler. Pat influenced the field of chemical dependency treatment in local, state, national, and international arenas.

In addition to business competence, Pat also learned through his father the importance of creating a supportive, respectful, and emotionally safe working environment for all employees. A deeply fair and honest man, Pat not only knew and cared about each person who worked for Hazelden, he also created and nourished an environment in which employees felt free enough to experiment and to fail. This is not to say that Pat liked failure; he didn't. Pat did understand, however, that it takes trial and error to develop a good idea. Hazelden's rise to a preeminent role in the addictions treatment field during Pat's era was due in large part to this positive work atmosphere. Pat also understood that one person can't run an organization. He deliberately recruited other strong, capable leaders; Daniel

Anderson and Harry Swift are typical examples, and he gave them the authority to do their jobs.

Pat's respect for the dignity of the individual included each person who sought Hazelden's services. It is also thanks to Pat's leadership that Hazelden has always sought to treat patients with respect and to provide a warm, nurturing atmosphere in which they can heal and grow. In addition, his unrelenting work on the national stage helped change society's view of alcoholics as "immoral degenerates" to that of individuals with an uncontrolled illness who deserve respect and help. Underlying all of Pat's work was one goal: to help suffering alcoholics, and to do so with love and understanding.

Pat Butler, 1983. "A man of great energy . . . a person with a great sensitivity for people and a feeling for the community . . . a faithful friend with a marvelous sense of humor . . . a devoted husband and loving father with a radiant smile . . . a man of the utmost integrity."

PROLOGUE

It was a cloudless, uncharacteristically cool day July 31, 1990, as an uncommonly large gathering of people filled the Cathedral of St. Paul to participate in the Catholic liturgy celebrating the death and rising of the ninety-year-old Patrick Butler. If the Greek philosopher Diogenes were still searching with his lantern for the one man of integrity, his search would have ended with the scrutiny of the life of Patrick Butler.

It was truly an ecumenical gathering. Representatives of the Catholic and Protestant clergy filled the sanctuary, while a large cross-section of the Minnesota lay community filled the huge nave of the cathedral. As Archbishop John Roach eulogized the gifted, gentle, and gracious St. Paulite, those in the immense crowd silently searched their souls for the words to describe this venerable man who had personally touched the lives of so many people. Many remembered how his charismatic personality manifested itself in their own lives. A man of great energy, a lively conversationalist, a person with a great sensitivity for people and a feeling for the community, a Christian delighted and enthusiastic about life itself, a faithful friend with a marvelous sense of humor, a devoted husband and loving father with a radiant smile, a member of the fellowship of Alcoholics Anonymous (AA) who genuinely cared about people in need, for whom he was gracious and generous, a charming host, an exuberant and delightful storyteller, a person after whom one could model oneself, and the person whom Diogenes had been searching for—a man of the utmost integrity.

I truly believe that Pat didn't really like being in the spotlight. He was the kind of person who led in a way that people didn't really know they were being led—a particularly effective style of leadership to use with alcoholics, I might add!

—WARREN M.

Patrick Butler

A BIOGRAPHY

Part One: Before Treatment

Pat Butler in 1910

Chapter 1

ANCESTORS AND CHILDHOOD

Patrick Butler was born on October 18, 1900. He was the third child and the second son of R. Emmett Butler and Louisa Biggs, named after his grandfather, Patrick, who emigrated from Ireland in 1852. To appreciate Pat Butler's genius, creativity, grace, and special signature that he left on the unique endeavors upon which he embarked, one must have some insights into the character of the Butler family, particularly his father, Emmett, and his grandfather, Patrick, of whose six sons Emmett was the last.

Grandfather Butler was born in 1823, the son of a poor Irish tenant farmer, near Dublin in the township of Balinhinch, County Wicklow. Oral tradition suggests (the records cannot confirm it) that he graduated from Trinity College in Dublin in 1846 as a civil engineer. True or not, he was highly proficient in mathematics—a skill that he taught all his children. As Ireland suffered through the aftermath of the horrible potato famine, Patrick, like so many other Irish men and women, decided to emigrate to America.

Arriving in 1852, he settled first in Pennsylvania, where he worked

Pat's grandfather, Patrick Butler (1823–1900). His knowledge of mathematics was a decisive factor in his sons' becoming shrewd businessmen.
Mary Ann Gaffney Butler, Pat's grandmother (1830–1915)

as a farmhand, and later moved to Galena, Illinois, where he met and married Mary Ann Gaffney in 1855. The following year the two of them trekked to Minnesota, eventually settling in Waterford, Dakota County, in 1862, where they acquired 320 acres of farmland. As a farmer he had good harvests and failures, but one crop that never failed was his children—there were nine, six boys and three girls, from Catherine, the oldest, who was born in 1855, to the youngest, Effie, who was born twenty years later.

It was a very close-knit, hardworking, frugal, and industrious family. The early education of the children took place in a one-room schoolhouse supplemented at home by their father's knowledge of mathematics, a decisive factor in the sons' becoming shrewd businessmen. The boys were not reluctant to use their fists to defend themselves and their religion, particularly since they were the only Irish Catholic family in the area. Prejudice and intolerance against Catholics and immigrants was especially strong in the United States in the mid-1800s. On one occasion a petition was circulated to keep the Butler children out of the school. However, with threats and a severe tongue-lashing, Pat Butler got the board members to halt the proceedings.

The family's religious needs were administered to by a priest who visited the area every few months. Irish transients could always find some food and shelter with the Butlers, poor though they were. Everyone in the family had to work and do some chores. Emmett remembered milking cows with his brother Pierce and, day after day, hearing Pierce on his milking stool reciting long passages of Shakespeare from memory. Pierce was the exception among the boys, all of whom got into construction. But Pierce also studied law and later was appointed a justice of the Supreme Court in 1923 by President Warren Harding. At Carleton College his best subject was rhetoric. He almost flunked constitutional law, which ordinarily would have presaged an unsuitability for the highest judicial office that he was destined to attain.

Grandfather Patrick Butler was known for his temper and was prepared to fight at the drop of a hat. The fact that his adversary was not an Irishman or a Catholic was sufficient justification for a fight any day. He was a great wrestler and never saw the day that any of his sons could pin him. The sons also experienced his temper, and their mother had to remonstrate with him to be more gentle with them lest they leave home.

But eventually for economic reasons they did leave home. One by one, beginning with the eldest, Walter, they relocated to St. Paul, where they got into construction, starting with the bricklaying trade. In time Walter, William, John, and Cooley formed one of the best and most renowned companies in the Midwest, called Butler Brothers. To mention but a few of their outstanding achievements, Butler Brothers built the State Capitol in St. Paul, the Michigan Central Railway tunnel under the Detroit River, the ore docks on Lake Superior, and a section of the Grand Central Station in New York. The last to become a full partner in the business was the youngest, Emmett, who threatened to set up his own business unless he were treated as an equal and not just as an employee of Butler Brothers.

John Butler, the second eldest, sensed the great opportunities that the mining industry might hold for an entrepreneurial company such as the Butlers. In 1902 he went to the wilderness of the Mesabi Range, where he signed lucrative strip-mining contracts. He probably did not realize that he was shaping the destiny of Butler Brothers. In the coming decades his creative mind, together with that of his brother Emmett, would initiate a series of innovations in the mining industry just as he and his brothers had done earlier in the field of construction. He eventually prevailed upon Butler Brothers to move from construction to mining, although Walter was always interested in the construction business and eventually formed his own company.

John's timing was perfect. The first decade of the twentieth century was the beginning of the steel age in modern history. No one ever suspected it then, but the availability of high-grade, low-cost iron from the sprawling pits of Mesabi and other ranges in northern Minnesota was to become the most important single factor in making the United States a world power, for the world would be crying for steel. Between 1905 and 1907 thirty thousand men were imported from the Balkan States to the Mesabi Range. At one time Butler Brothers had nationals from thirty-two foreign countries on the payroll.

In 1908 John was joined by Emmett, who took over the Sliver Mine and settled in Nashwauk, a small town between Grand Rapids and Hibbing. The two brothers led busy lives, usually living at the mine locations and traveling back and forth among the mines by horse and buggy. Emmett's daughter, Mary Ellen, reminiscing about her early summers on the range, recalled, "I can still see father trudging along the railroad tracks in suspenders, his shirt sleeves rolled up and his shoulders bent in concentration. The stoop in his shoulders was always an indication whether things were going well or badly."

Emmett and John were impatient of stupidity, and Emmett particularly had a foul temper with the men when things were not going

*Pat's father, Emmett Butler (1870–1955), in 1910 at the
Sliver Mine, Virginia, Minnesota*

smoothly. At the same time they were extremely fond of and loyal to their employees. They recognized from the outset that the success of Butler Brothers depended on the men hired to help them, and they did not expect more of the workers than they did of themselves.

Emmett's wife, Louisa, followed him to Nashwauk, accompanied by their four children: Mary Ellen (born 1895), Hazen (born 1897), Patrick (born 1900), and Lawrence Michael (born 1903). Cooley would be born in 1914. Patrick was born in St. Paul on Virginia Avenue, south of University Avenue. His grandfather had just died some months previous to his birth in 1900, and this was probably the main reason that he was baptized Patrick. For a while he was called Tim, the name he assumed when he was confirmed by Archbishop John Ireland. The name never caught on, however, and he soon reverted to Pat. At his confirmation, Pat promised that he would not drink alcohol, a pledge that he kept until he went to college. In 1906 the family moved to Hague and Dunlop avenues where Mary Ellen, Hazen, and Pat attended St. Luke's parochial school.

When the family moved to Nashwauk in 1908, Louisa Butler would drive the children to school in Virginia in a horse and buggy over very difficult terrain. Mary Ellen recalled that there were more than twenty-three nationalities in the school. She also noted, "I can remember we passed nineteen saloons in five blocks to get there. Hogs, cows, and chickens roamed the streets."

Emmett and Louisa quickly decided that the children would be better off going to school in St. Paul. The following year, 1909, Hazen and Patrick were enrolled in the preparatory school at the College of St. Thomas, where they boarded. Mary Ellen went to Derham Hall and then to Visitation Convent for high school. They rejoined their parents for

Pat's grandmother, Ellen Hammond Biggs (seated), and his mother, Louisa Biggs Butler (standing in back). The children pictured are (right to left) Mary Ellen, Hazen, Patrick, Lawrence Michael. Photo taken in 1905.

summers and holidays. Their mother worked hard keeping house, a vegetable garden, chickens, and horses. After three years, their parents relocated to Virginia, still a thriving lumber center with two or three large lumber mills. In 1920 the family returned permanently to St. Paul, residing at 448 River Road.

In the summers Hazen and Pat learned the mining business, either from doing a variety of tasks in the mines or from their father while accompanying him on his inspections. Mary Ellen worked at the office at Nashwauk. Pat had a horse named Maggie that he liked to display and show off. But pride goeth before the fall. On one occasion when Pat was riding to fetch the company mail, Maggie decided to wade into some shallow water and rolled over in it, muddying her rider and soaking the mail.

St. Thomas, where Hazen and Patrick boarded during the school year, was run by the archdiocese of St. Paul, which at that time owned all of the land west of the campus to the Mississippi River. The students could walk all the way to Fort Snelling on college property, encountering the territorial roads now called Snelling and Cleveland avenues but very few buildings. St. Thomas was originally set up as a military preparatory school, and the students had to wear uniforms. At St. Thomas, Pat preferred history to all his other subjects. He liked sports, played second base in baseball, and quarterbacked the Mohawks, the name of one of the intramural football teams at the school. He was also called upon to play second-string quarterback on the varsity football team after some of the players enlisted when the United States entered the First World War in 1917.

Pat was fond of music. His father recalled that about the second year that Pat was at St. Thomas, one of the teachers who taught music

Hazen and Patrick Butler as St. Thomas cadets, 1911,
St. Paul, Minnesota

"wanted to make a violin player out of Pat. I came home one night and Pat was sawing away on the violin. I said, 'Son, if you want to saw on that damn thing, get out to the water tower and work on it there and not in the house.' Pat never learned to play the violin." Pat was very shy and timid as well as sensitive as a youngster. Some of his mother's friends described him as very pretty when he was posing for a picture, which Hazen happened to overhear. When Hazen teased his younger brother as the pretty boy in the family, Patrick started to cry and stammered, "I can't help it if I'm pretty."

Pat graduated from high school at St. Thomas in June 1917. Most of his classmates went on to seminary. Although at an early age he had decided he wanted to be a bishop (whether he thought he could skip the priesthood isn't clear), Pat decided upon Yale University instead, where he would major in history. His advisor at St. Thomas suggested that he first take a year of college at St. Thomas, which he did. It was a cagey move, as it allowed him to transfer into the freshman class at Yale in January 1918 without having to take the entrance exams. Pat was not sure whether he would have passed them.

He was somewhat lonely in his first two years at Yale, as most of his classmates already had established friendships, coming from the same East Coast prep schools, especially Phillips Academy in Andover, Massachusetts, and Phillips Exeter Academy in Exeter, New Hampshire. With the help of alcohol, however, he overcame his social shyness and made some good friends in his junior and senior years. He was put on the scrub football team that scrimmaged with the varsity. As a reward in his senior year, he was allowed to play a few minutes against Harvard. Besides studying history he also made history, for he was the first player to break his leg in the Yale Bowl playing against

Pat's parents, Emmett and Louisa, in Tucson, Arizona, 1953. Pat's deep, abiding love for his parents was transferred to the extended Butler family as he assumed the role of beloved and trusted patriarch.

Harvard. Otherwise his years at college were uneventful—even his drinking, although it did cause him some embarrassment when he passed out at his friend's wedding and once got himself into trouble with the law. But those things were not unexpected from college students, despite the fact that the rules of Prohibition were supposedly enforced. He graduated Alpha Delta Phi from Yale University with a bachelor of philosophy in June 1922.

That same summer Pat took a trip to Europe with a classmate on the SS *Regina,* out of Montreal. He was immediately attracted to another passenger named Aimee Mott—a freshman at Vassar, a striking and charming young lady. He had the opportunity to have a number of conversations with her on the ship and then arranged his itinerary mostly to coincide with hers during the two months that she was abroad. Aimee recalled that Pat had a great sense of humor and was fun to be with. For his part Pat was very much taken with the tall, young brunette. When they returned to the United States, they corresponded with one another, and Aimee invited him to her family's home near Flint, Michigan, during her holidays from school. Pat, in turn, would occasionally come east to take her to one of the Yale football games.

Chapter 2

Butler Brothers —
Mining and Construction Magnates

When Pat returned from the summer trip to Europe, he spent the next year and a half with his cousin Leo Butler (Pierce's son), building roads in Iowa and Illinois, and then resumed working with his father at the Cuyuna Range in 1924. Pat did not go back to working with his father immediately upon his return from Europe in the fall of 1922 because Emmett had left the mining operation after a falling-out with his brothers and had returned to the business of building roads. Being the youngest, he had always felt that he was being treated like a second-class citizen by his older brothers. Older brothers do have a tendency of not taking the youngest seriously and may have been a little jealous of him.

By the end of 1923, however, John, who was primarily responsible for moving Butler Brothers into the lucrative mining business, had become too weak to continue physical labor. Walter and John consequently asked Emmett to return in 1924 and take full charge of the mining operations, which Emmett had made a condition of his return. Walter wasn't pleased with Emmett's attitude, but he had never been too happy with the mining business and would soon withdraw to form his own construction corporation.

Emmett then decided to send Pat to manage the Butler Brothers Cleveland office, where Pat dealt with the agents responsible for selling the iron ore from the mines in Minnesota. In those early years the agents were the Hanna Mining Company and Pickard's Mather and Company, who represented U.S. Steel, Bethlehem Steel, and Republic Steel, among others. Of course, Pat was only too happy to go to Cleveland because it was a lot closer than St. Paul was to Aimee's home in Flint.

John died in 1926 and left all his Butler Brothers' stock to Pierce, which did not settle well with Walter and precipitated the latter's decision to sell Butler Brothers, a move that Emmett opposed. Relations between Emmett and Walter had long been strained, and Walter's decision to sell was a further cause for the deterioration of the relationship between the youngest and the oldest brothers. Emmett wanted to keep the business in the family, while Walter wanted to sell it to get the money, all the time refusing to pay the federal government the taxes that were owed. Finally, Walter offered to sell his stock to Emmett for $1.8 million. In order for the deal with Walter to go through, Emmett became vitally dependent on the contracts in Cleveland with the big steel companies. All this was taking place just as the Great Depression was about to hit the U.S. economy.

Fortunately, the depression that began in 1929 would not hit the steel industry for another year or two. Pat told the story of his first visit to the New York Stock Exchange the day the market took its first huge tumble. He and a friend were in New York attending a convention sponsored by U.S. Steel and they managed to get onto the floor of the stock exchange. They thought that the people were going insane because of their frantic behavior, discovering only the next day what had really occurred. The ticker tapes had been two hours behind, signaling the beginning of the great crash.

Despite the start of the crash, 1929 was the best year in the history of Butler Brothers. The company shipped more than 2.3 million tons of iron ore to Cleveland, the most ever. It did not suffer too badly in 1930, and 1931 could have been worse. But in 1932 the depression really hit hard; every company that had a contract with Butler Brothers sent notice that they wouldn't take any more ore. Emmett Butler was broke. President Franklin Roosevelt was elected to his first term that same year, but despite his inaugural speech, in which he stated, "The only thing we have to fear is fear itself," Emmett did not know where the money would come from to pay his bills, especially those from Walter, who kept suing him so that he would default and sell the company.

In 1932 Emmett went to Cleveland to assist his son and to play hardball with the steel companies, which had canceled their contracts. There were seven of them, including U.S. Steel, Republic, and Bethlehem. Before the meeting Emmett had scheduled with representatives from each of the seven clients, he had taken one of the representatives aside and threatened that he would sue every one of them for everything in the book, "from pregnancy to nervous prostration." At the meeting all twenty representatives said that they could not make use of the iron ore because business was so slow and they would not take any more ore from Butler Brothers. Emmett remonstrated that he had contracts with every one of them. All they had to do was simply take the minimum specified by the contract

In the throes of the Great Depression, Emmett Butler played hardball with big steel companies and kept Butler Brothers solvent. At the time, son Patrick had doubts about his ability to replicate his father's business acumen and tenacity.

and he would be able to survive financially. He offered to put the ore anyplace they wanted it.

Emmett's nephew Pierce Butler Jr. (a lawyer like his father Pierce) was in Cleveland that day and got word of his uncle's plight. Emmett related that "Pierce was coming off a hangover just enough to be belligerent as hell." At the meeting Pierce accused the company representatives of collusion, and "they got as red as hell." At lunch one of the representatives of Republic Steel tried to get Emmett drunk, ordering three pails of dry martinis. But Emmett would have none of it. In the afternoon an old lawyer representing Republic Steel who had listened quietly all day finally got out of his chair and pronounced, "Gentlemen, we owe Butler Brothers enough under these contracts to keep them solvent, and I advise you to arrange it so that they can live." That won the day for Emmett and ended the meeting.

Pat, not as hard-nosed as his father, learned some valuable lessons that day, one of which was not to drink at lunch when there was serious business to be done. He also learned not to be bullied by numbers and names and observed that his father had a deep care and concern for his employees—something that Pat would carry over into his second career. His awe and admiration for his father increased that day, as well as his doubts about himself and his ability to replicate his father's business acumen and tenacity.

Despite the somewhat satisfactory resolution of the contracts with the steel companies, 1933 was a very difficult year for Butler Brothers. The company barely kept going, with the men at the mine doing odd jobs. But Emmett was determined to uphold the commitment he had made to his employees a decade before, when he had returned to take charge of the mining operations. At that time, he put out a memorandum that no one was to be discharged if they had been doing their work. Foremen were to find jobs that the men could do. His attitude was that these men had given many years of their lives to Butler Brothers and unless they did something wrong and against the rules, they were entitled to be taken care of by the organization. Emmett noted, "That made for more loyalty as no one felt he was going to be canned because he was getting old. The surprising thing was that everyone did more work than they did before, because they felt and believed that they were being treated right." Of course Walter did not think that this was good business and opposed the little outlay involved.

The year 1934 was a reasonably good one, and by 1937 Butler Brothers were out of trouble. In 1939 the Second World War started and the steel industry could not get enough iron ore. That was when Pat returned to St. Paul to help his father, becoming vice president in charge of business operations. In this role Pat ran the business during the booming and lucrative years of World War II.

at was also an extremely good businessperson. Part of that skill has to be attributed to his ability and willingness to listen to others when he was working on a problem. Just as he never held himself above other Fellowship Club residents, he never held himself above those he worked with in business. Speaking from my experience as a member of the Hazelden Board of Trustees, I know that Pat sincerely wanted to know what we thought about issues, and he paid attention. He made everyone feel that they were involved and that their opinion mattered—and it did. To Pat, everyone mattered.

—JON OLSON

've worked for Hazelden for twenty years, and in the early days of my employment, Pat was what I would call Hazelden's "Rock of Gibraltar." He had a keen interest not only in Hazelden, but also in how the steps of AA and the traditions of AA would be adhered to by an organization that was growing by leaps and bounds.

Every Tuesday, wearing his trademark small hat and carrying a twenty-nine-cent shopping bag, Pat was here on Hazelden's campus. He was chairman of the board at the time, and, being quite new to the organization, I only knew of him—and I was aware that he'd done a lot for Hazelden. I remember being quite surprised to see him one day eating in the cafeteria with the staff. I guess I mentioned this to a colleague, only to learn that Pat preferred to eat, not in the board room, but with the employees. This was one of the first clues I had that Pat was someone unusual and special.

Some time later, I was working for Hazelden as a consultant to small and medium sized businesses and industries helping them set up employee assistance programs. I considered myself a "lowly" guy in the organization, and it was in this context that I was called on one day to meet with the Hazelden board to report on our project's progress. Pat was there, of course, and with his camera, too. I hadn't yet been introduced to his photography habit, and was rather surprised when Pat took my picture. I didn't really think too much of it until, about three weeks after the meeting, I received that photo in the mail together with a short note from Pat that said something like, "Great to meet with you!" I can tell you that this made me feel like a million dollars. It was something so unexpected—a note and photo to me of all people, from the chairman of the board! Over time, of course, I discovered that Pat regularly made such gestures, and that they truly came from his heart.

Pat was one of the most humble and unassuming people I've ever met. The day the board named "Pat Butler Drive" after Pat, for example, they had to suspend him from the board for twenty-four hours. Why? Because they knew he would never have allowed a vote to do this to go forward.

Perhaps my fondest memory is of Pat's enduring commitment to this organization. Pat had enough money to do whatever he wanted with his life, yet he chose to focus his life and means on helping suffering alcoholics. His goal was synonymous with Hazelden's: how can we most effectively help the greatest number of people. Pat was always clear that Hazelden was here for one reason: to treat the patient. That's his ongoing legacy to us.

—GARY HESTNESS

Chapter 3

MARRIAGE, FAMILY, AND POLITICS

In addition to launching his business career, Pat's move to Cleveland also brought him a lot closer to Aimee Mott. She was the daughter of Charles Stewart Mott, who helped build General Motors (GM) into the world's largest corporation and later dispersed his wealth for the benefit of the people in his community of Flint, Michigan. Mott was considered one of the richest men in the world through his ownership of some four million shares of GM stock. As a result Aimee was a wealthy woman in her own right. Aimee's father was a very reticent and quiet man when not engaged with his work. Pat was not at ease with him and dreaded going riding with him, as he would go for hours without conversation.

Aimee was a tall girl even when she was young. Her father would embarrass her when he took her to the movies by insisting that she receive the children's price. Because of her height she was accustomed to take the lead in dancing when she was in college. This caused problems for Pat since he could only dance, and not that well, if he were the leader.

Aimee Mott Butler, 1929, at the age of 27

Aimee Mott Butler and daughter, Kate

In 1925 Pat Butler and Aimee Mott became engaged while she was in her senior year at Vassar. Pat bought Aimee a sapphire stone for an engagement ring, which both he and the woman who sold it to him liked very much. But Aimee didn't. Although she never told Pat, there were times when she did not wear it, hoping that he would notice and ask her about it. But Pat was oblivious to its absence. Several years later, however, when she got really angry with him during his heavy drinking, she turned it in. Fortunately for Pat, she was very pleased with the wedding ring.

They were married on May 29, 1926. They had to get a dispensation for a mixed marriage because Aimee was Episcopalian. In those days mixed marriages could not be performed in a church, so the wedding (presided over by Father Pat Gallagher) and reception were held on the grounds of the Mott home in Applewood, a small town near Flint. A beautiful day with the lilacs in full bloom, the wedding of Aimee Mott and Patrick Butler was the social event of the year for miles around. The self-made Irishman, Emmett, like his son, had difficulty finding common ground for conversation with C. S. Mott.

Pat was diplomatic enough to borrow a GM-made Buick from a friend of his in the wedding party to begin the honeymoon rather than leave in his Chrysler, an arch rival of GM. The newlyweds spent a week in New York near Poughkeepsie and then returned to Cleveland for the beginning of the ore-mining season. Once the press of business was over they returned to Europe in the fall, visiting Florence and Paris. The following February they returned to Cleveland, where they rented a home until they built their own in suburban Shaker Heights.

The Butler family at their Summit Avenue home in St. Paul, 1941. Seated in Pat's lap is daughter, Kate. Patrick Jr., Peter, and their mother, Aimee, look on. Also pictured is the family dog, Pepsi.

Pat and Aimee's first two children, young Pat and his brother, Peter, were born about fourteen months apart, in 1930 and 1931, respectively. Their father was very fond of his children, and Katherine (Kate), born in 1940 after the family returned to St. Paul, became the apple of his eye. He treated the boys as if they were twins. When the two were very young, Pat was the more aggressive one, often trying to climb into Peter's playpen to wrestle with his younger sibling. As they grew older, their father would take them to his office at the capitol and show them the many sights of Cleveland. Visits to the amusement park, boating on Lake Erie, and winters in Bermuda, Jamaica, and Florida were fond memories.

These happy and early years were not without concerns, as Aimee began to experience recurring waves of depression. The letters from Aimee to her father reveal the love and care she had for her children despite these difficult periods. The children's needs were seen to by a governess during Aimee's protracted illnesses and Pat's absences occasioned by his many business trips.

Pat wasn't rough on the boys, who were extremely fond of their father. As they grew older they would fight a lot, as brothers usually do. Finally, Pat got the two of them boxing gloves and told them to go at one another. After a short time, they got weary of it and begged him to let them stop—but he wouldn't. He made them continue until they were exhausted and couldn't lift their little arms anymore. From then on, whenever the squabbling became too much for the parents, all Pat would have to do would be to threaten them with the boxing gloves. His harshest form of punishment was to slap the palm of their hands. When young Patrick withdrew his once to avoid the strike, his father made him memorize the Gettysburg Address.

*Patrick Butler, state representative, Cleveland, Ohio, 1935.
In those days, the fun of politics consisted a great deal in
finding kindred souls with similar drinking habits. At
heart, Pat was not a politician.*

Pat liked to tease his sons, but oftentimes the boys gave as good as they received. One time when Pat asked little Pat to show him his muscle, young Pat retorted, "What do you expect me to be—a Tarzan—just because you bore me?" As he became older, he became quite outspoken. One time he said to his dad, "At the party this evening please don't tell those old jokes. Nobody laughs at them."

Another time when young Pat was about ten years old, his father remarked at Sunday dinner that all the children would be independently wealthy. Young Patrick quickly asked, "Well, where is it?"

Patrick senior replied, "Ask your grandfather."

Young Patrick ran to the phone, called his grandfather, and got him away from the dinner table to ask him about the money. C. S. Mott handled it pretty well, at least to young Patrick's satisfaction.

During the lean years of the thirties when the ore-mining business was very slow, Pat had time to get into politics. He was elected to the Ohio state legislature in 1934. He served two two-year terms in the house of representatives as a Democrat during the Roosevelt years. The principal reason that he did not run again was because business had picked up, although a certain amount of boredom had also set in. At heart Pat was not really a politician. Moreover, the fun of politics, if not the business, consisted a great deal in finding kindred souls with similar drinking habits. His young son Patrick astutely remarked once that the state-controlled liquor store was where his father bought liquor and made politics. By the end of his tenure Pat found that he was a conservative at heart and had more in common with the Republicans than with the members of his own party. He liked Roosevelt well enough until he became thoroughly disenchanted with the president's decision to run for a third term. While

Pat's tenure in the Ohio state legislature was relatively short, he gained the political savvy necessary later for pursuing his life's mission in Minnesota.

In 1939 when Pat returned to St. Paul to work as vice president for his father, he settled his family at 370 Summit Avenue, which remained their home for close to thirty-five years. A beautiful, spacious Georgian home, it was built in 1912 and had three floors. They were in the parish boundaries of the Cathedral of St. Paul. Whenever he was at home, Pat would attend the 6 A.M. Mass. Often on cold winter mornings when the altar boy failed to appear, Pat would come forward, open the two bronze gates, and serve the newly assigned priest, Father James Shannon, who became very close to the Butler family. Pat's two sons, who attended St. Paul Academy, were in Father Shannon's confirmation class. Father Shannon and Peter both attended Yale in the fifties, Peter as an undergraduate and Shannon as a graduate student. Later Father Shannon would serve as the president of the College of St. Thomas.

at was a completely nonjudgmental person. He respected others' ideas, and he could take in and sift opinions and information without ego involvement. It was his openness and humility that allowed him to do that. Pat didn't have to be right; he just wanted to see the merit, or lack thereof, of an idea come out. He was always willing to give up ownership.

Pat was such a radiant man. Somehow, Pat managed to preserve that initial appreciation you get when you're first sober and you've just turned your life around. To me he modeled sobriety better than anyone I've ever known. He had contented, happy, generous sobriety. It was always there, whenever I saw him, regardless of the context. He turned his life over and then just kept doing so for the rest of his life.

—ELAINE WALKER

Chapter 4

PROGRESSION OF AN ILLNESS

Besides raising his family, engaging in politics, and marketing Butler Brothers iron ore, Pat Butler was afflicted with an illness that over the course of some thirty years became progressively worse. His father's generation of Butlers was known as a drinking family. Emmett's children inherited and cultivated their father's habit and continued the family tradition. The genetic connection appears quite conclusive. Although their mother, Louisa, did not like her husband's excessive drinking, she did not nag him about it. When her sons still lived at home, she would send them to get their father from the local tavern when he was late arriving home. Everyone in town knew that the Butlers had a drinking problem. Nor were they the only Irish family in St. Paul that had one.

On his fourteenth birthday, Pat's Aunt Kate, the matriarch of the Butler family, gave him an umbrella with the exhortation: "I hope that you will always keep dry." She wasn't just talking about the rain, Pat remembered. Pat took his first drink when he was eighteen and recalled that it gave him quite a lift. He was just beginning college the same year that the U.S. Constitution was amended by the Volstead Act and Prohibition became the law of the land. However, it did little to discourage, much less end, the drinking habits of Americans. Alcohol was still easy to obtain.

Drinking at many colleges remained extensive, and Pat did his share. He had a lot of hangovers, made a fool of himself at a friend's wedding as well as on other occasions that he did not even remember, and found himself in trouble with the law a few times. Hundreds of other college students went through similar experiences. Besides, the drinking helped him overcome his shyness and strengthened his social skills. Drinking in college was a rite of passage for many students. Pat started to smoke about the same time that he began drinking. The problem for Pat was that the rite of passage did not end with his graduation from college. On the contrary, over the years the drinking got progressively worse.

After his marriage in 1926, Pat continued his drinking ways. Aimee didn't know what the problem was, especially since she didn't drink herself and had no experience of it in her own family. Pat was a binge drinker, and when these sessions occurred, he would disappear either at home or on a business trip. Occasionally, after her husband had been drinking around the clock and went to sleep it off, she would hide the bottles. (Later, in St. Paul, she would hide his shoes, hoping to keep him from leaving the house to go to a bar.) But hiding bottles soon proved useless.

Once when driving the 220 miles from Cleveland to Flint with the two boys in the car, they stopped at a coffee shop. Pat left to get something but never returned. Aimee was frantic, waited and waited, and finally got in the car with the children and drove to Flint by herself, not knowing what else to do. The next day a contrite Pat called and pleaded with Aimee to fetch him. He had stopped in a bar to get a drink and that was the last that he remembered.

Pat began to recognize in Cleveland that he had a problem, especially when, after drinking with his politician buddies, he would continually wake up with a hangover even worse than the previous one. During these years in Cleveland while the boys were growing up, Pat went to seek help a couple of times but the sanatoriums selected were little more than drying out places. One of them used the aversion treatment, which, while it made Pat sick, had no lasting effect. Others suggested hobbies like bookbinding, billiards, golf, and flying, all of which occupied Pat for a time but not to the neglect of his drinking. For the most part Pat was a solitary drinker and a quiet drunk who rarely made a public display of himself and who never became mean-spirited except for a sharp tongue, which became even more caustic when he drank.

When Pat moved back to St. Paul in 1939, he thought the geographic change would help moderate his drinking, but it did not. He received little or no help from his family. His father was still spending long evenings at the St. Paul Athletic Club, his brothers continued to drink, and no one seemed inclined to stop, nor did anyone know how. It was just the "Irish disease." Alcoholics Anonymous (AA) was in its infancy and, in 1939, still unknown in Minnesota. A year later, however, AA arrived in the Twin Cities in the person of B. Patrick Cronin, a contemporary of Patrick Butler.

Cronin's drinking had cost him job after job and by the age of thirty-six he had become a full-fledged alcoholic. Then in the early summer of 1940, the year after Pat and his family had settled in St.

Paul, Cronin read a review of the Big Book, *Alcoholics Anonymous*, published in 1939. He wrote to the General Service Office of Alcoholics Anonymous in New York, inquiring whether Minneapolis had any AA members. He received a negative response with the suggestion that he could contact the strong AA Fellowship in Chicago.

Eventually, two Chicago natives to whom his name had been given barged in on Cronin on November 9, 1940. The catastrophic Black Blizzard of 1940 began the next day, delaying their departure, providing them with four days to "work on" Cronin, whose dry date was November 11, 1940. Ever since that time the grateful Cronin's influence on the growth of AA throughout the Midwest was preeminent—approximately 450 AA groups trace their establishment to his direct or indirect influence.

Emmett started going to one of these groups in 1945. His recovery was very important to him, and with it he once again started going to the sacraments in the Catholic Church. He then began to urge his sons to go to AA meetings to do something about their excessive drinking. One by one they gradually heeded his advice. Hazen, the oldest and the son upon whom Emmett had been the hardest, stopped drinking on his own without going to AA. Larry went to Hazelden as its first patient in April 1949, and became a member of the board of trustees the following year. It took a little longer for Pat. Back in 1941, when Aimee had shown him an article about AA in the *Saturday Evening Post*, Pat had remarked that AA might be a help to his brother Larry, who really had a drinking problem.

Following his father's counsel and example, Pat did try a few AA meetings, traveling over to Minneapolis where he thought he wouldn't be recognized. He didn't want anyone to know that he had a problem, although most of his friends and acquaintances in St. Paul knew that he did. But he wasn't ready to stop drinking and the visits to Minneapolis did not continue for any length of time. Occasionally, after a stint in a hospital or sanatorium, Pat would go on the wagon and his friends and family would heave a collective sigh of relief hoping that this period of not drinking would last a little longer than the last time.

When he did drink heavily, Pat would disappear in the house and sleep it off or go to the hospital to be detoxed. The diagnosis would be for a nervous disorder. Otherwise these dances with intoxication would occur on business trips. But Pat continued to play a role in the lives of his children, and he took extra care not to be around his daughter, Kate, who was born in 1940, when he was drinking.

In 1947 Pat took his two boys with him to celebrate the twenty-fifth anniversary of his graduation from Yale and proceeded to make a spectacle of himself with his drinking. While the boys often did see their father inebriated, especially in the mid- to late-forties, his drinking was not a major factor in their lives and apparently was not a source of unhappiness for them. He shared their interest in sports and would organize softball games for his sons and the neighbors. In her own way Aimee was always there for the boys as well, despite her illness, getting involved in their school activities, buying their clothes, and calling upon Pat to discipline them when they needed it and he was sober. Pat also took the boys with him on retreats to St. John's University in Collegeville or to the Jesuit retreat house on Lake Demontreville, which opened in 1948.

Pat's drinking became very alarming between 1948 and 1950. It would seem that a major reason for this was the idleness and boredom that set in when Butler Brothers was sold to the Hanna Mining Company. Pat had been running the company since his return from Cleveland. Hazen, who was no longer interested in the mining business, had already left the company. Leo and Francis, Pierce's sons, had been urging Emmett to sell, which he did in 1948. Pat, however, kept his stock in the company and used it to start the Butler Family Foundation in 1950. At the age of forty-eight Pat was a retired millionaire. Having nothing to do, he turned to drinking more frequently and more heavily.

By 1948 he knew that his drinking was out of control and he was desperate to do something about it. He was drinking without any excuses. In these years of his heaviest drinking he turned more and more to religion for the cure to his alcoholism, not comprehending what the nature of the problem truly was.

In 1949 Pat went to a psychiatric hospital in Milwaukee but remained only until he had dried out. His father and his brother Larry prevailed upon him to go to Hazelden in January 1950. He stayed only a few days and returned to Florida where his family was wintering. He was miserable in his sobriety, which was short-lived. He prayed for help, but subconsciously he wanted to be tempted beyond his strength, and that was the prayer that was answered. He resumed his drinking and drank heavily until July 1950, when he returned to Hazelden. There he followed the simple treatment model that subsequently would have a tremendous impact throughout the United States: he made his bed along with everyone else, acted like a gentleman, was educated in the Twelve Steps and the problem and the solution (something that none of the sanatoriums had offered), and shared his story with the other guests at Hazelden. When he left, he was careful to follow the instructions of his sponsor, Lynn Carroll, about attending meetings, not drinking, and doing a lot of Twelve Stepping. It was as simple as that. This time his sobriety was long-lived—forty years— and, instead of golf, flying, and bookbinding, his lifelong avocation was now helping other alcoholics.

As many people know, Pat was a regular at Fellowship Club for many years, and he loved to mingle and talk with the residents. I remember someone asking him once how one became an old-timer. His reply? "Live a long time and don't drink!" Pat was never hesitant to talk about his own struggles with alcohol and treatment when it seemed appropriate. He got sober, relapsed, and then went back into treatment again. I heard him tell someone once, after thirty-some years of sobriety, "When I went back into treatment a second time, the program had changed." Pat knew that the program hadn't changed a bit, of course. But he loved to tell the story anyway as a way, using himself as an example, to remind people that recovery is up to us, not up to a treatment center—and that even if people slip, they shouldn't give up.

—JON OLSON

Chapter 5

Spiritual Healing

W here are we to look for an explanation of the radical change that occurred in Pat Butler's life? A midlife crisis? Emancipation from his father's control and dominating personality? A conversion? The last is probably the best way of understanding it. But it needs some explanation.

Carl Jung, the famous Swiss psychiatrist, described alcoholism as a spiritual illness at the basis of which is one's yearning for wholeness. Jung described the journey toward wholeness as an individuation process. That process entails a struggle that is accomplished in stages as one works toward self-redemption and the wholeness of an undivided personality—an individual. The process has been aptly called a *heils-weg*, a healing or redemptive journey. This healing journey demands an overthrow of the existing order and the emergence of the real self. In a very real sense it is the mortal encounter between the two selves, a dominating theme in Western as well as Eastern thought. What Pat Butler had been experiencing was a radical example of the nature of crisis and the dying-rising theme that is at the heart of all spirituality.

*P*at could have drunk till he was nine hundred years old; he had enough money to do it. People could see that although Pat had a lot of money, he still couldn't afford to drink. Pat could show how you couldn't buy your way out of this kind of problem. The effect on heart and soul can't be denied, regardless of your financial station in life.

—WARREN M.

In the odyssey through life, everyone encounters crises that are both decisive and sacred. (Although it may be difficult to see Pat Butler's or any other alcoholic's pitiful plight as something sacred, it truly is.) A crisis contains an element of ambiguity and the person undergoing it does not know what will be decided. The negative side of the crisis evokes confusion and disorientation, which can come on suddenly, or it can emerge gradually and subtly. The person's normal way of seeing his or her identity begins to break down. The customary way of acting begins to crumble. The crisis is trying to tell the person that something has to be reorganized. It is a warning signal that an effort must be made to establish another method or approach to life. In a real sense a person in crisis experiences some part of himself or herself dying. A crisis can also be described as an emptying process.

The positive dimension of the crisis rests in the conscious awareness that, indeed, this disorientation is a very normal aspect of growth. God, or one's Higher Power, seeks through a crisis (or a sacred time) to draw us out of a controlled situation, and from the potency of the alcoholic disruption, disorder, even chaos, the positive, new attitude and behavior will erupt or emerge (the amount of pain will determine the verb used). The crisis pits one self against the other, the alcoholic self against the true self. One has to die. The rebirth, the renaissance, the rising follows from the dying, or the emptying. In that sense, every crisis is an analogous encounter with one's own mortality. Crisis is simply the way that humans grow, running counter to the myth that growth occurs in smooth, even steps in our journey. Crises are death rehearsals. If one hasn't rehearsed well, that person will go kicking and screaming into death.

Whether we use the analogy of heilsweg, or of life as a journey highlighted by crises, both contain the metaphor of dying and rising particularly applicable to the odyssey of the chemically dependent person.

The major obstacle for the alcoholic or the chemically dependent person is that he or she seeks to cut the journey short, to bypass or leap beyond the demands of the individuation process, and to become whole not through struggle and self-examination, not through the reconciliation of opposites, and especially not through the experience of pain and the death and rising of crisis situations—demands that life puts upon all of us. He or she wants to become whole without walking the heilsweg—the redemptive march. In this sense alcoholism is but a symptom of a more comprehensive *dis-ease* (discomfort), namely, one's search for self, for meaning, for wholeness.

What happened to Pat Butler in the years between 1948 and 1950 was that his alcoholic personality assumed control of his life. Pat had to recover his true personality, his true self, if he were going to survive. And the only way he could do that was to admit that he was powerless over alcohol, that he had an illness, that he could no longer control his drinking, and that he would have to abstain from alcohol. This was the nadir of his death-rising process, his heilsweg, his redemptive journey. The remainder of the journey, the recovery process, would continue for the rest of his life. And the rest of his life demonstrated his commitment to this recovery process. In all of his affairs, he practiced the principles that he learned during treatment. What had occurred was a personality change emerging on two levels. On one level he discovered and admitted that he was powerless to control his drinking. This change then manifested itself on another level, as he humbly asked God to remove his character defects—the intolerance, impatience, and caustic character of the alcoholic personality. These were replaced over the course of years with tolerance, patience, charity, and the gradual devolution of the fear, resentments, and self-centeredness of his alcoholic personality. Pierce III (the son of Pat's cousin Pierce Jr.) wrote that Pat "had probably, because of the brilliance of his father, a long and harrowing season of doubt about himself . . . of his ability to duplicate his father's creativity, but eventually he became more and more creative and did it in a far more difficult field."

I met Pat in 1954 when I first came into AA. This was the era when most everyone thought people drank too much because they had a weak will, bad morals, or both.

Pat and I and others all made a lot of calls on people who were looking for help to stop drinking. One place we went was the Willmar State Hospital. Besides Hazelden, that hospital was about the only place people could go to if they wanted someplace to dry out.

It wasn't unusual, either, for Pat and I to go to someone's home to talk about the disease of alcoholism. We went when we were asked—often by a wife, parent, brother or sister, or friend. Pat and I would go in, introduce ourselves, and say why we were there—that we understood that the person had a problem with alcohol. If he or she didn't deny this, we'd ask if we could talk to them for a while. We'd tell our own stories and explain the disease of alcoholism.

Pat was very good in these situations, in part, I believe, because he never talked down to anyone. He got across the point that we [alcoholics] weren't bad people and didn't mean to hurt people, yet we did. He explained how it was alcohol that led us into these actions, and that there was a program that could help us stay sober and avoid all this trouble.

— WARREN M.

Part Two: Recovery

Pat and Aimee Butler, 1968

Chapter 6

The Birth of Hazelden

The roots of Hazelden lay not with Pat Butler but rather with two disciples of Pat Cronin—Austin Ripley, a prominent newspaper writer and the famous author of *Minute Mysteries* and *Photo Crimes,* and Lynn Carroll, a lawyer and recovering alcoholic who would become Pat Butler's sponsor.

Ripley and Carroll, along with Robert McGarvey, owner of McGarvey's Coffee, were driven by a vision of a secluded place in the country where alcoholics could stay while the fog lifted and where they could absorb a little education about the illness from which they were suffering and about a way of recovering from it. About fifty miles north of the Twin Cities they found an isolated spot that was ideal for their purposes—a gentleman's farm, in a wooded lake area, far removed from urban distractions. They converted the manor into a treatment center affectionately known as the Old Lodge. The grounds then consisted of 217 acres of rolling land, some cultivated, some woodland, with about a mile of lakeshore on South Center Lake.

The birth of Hazelden originated from a vision of a secluded place, removed from urban disturbances, where alcoholics could stay while the fog lifted and where they could learn about their illness and about a way of recovering from it. The vision became a reality in the presence of the Old Lodge.

Hazelden opened in April 1949, with Lynn Carroll serving as director. His assistants were a cook who also served as a nurse, a maintenance man who cared for the external grounds, and a handyman who helped around the house and cared for the alcoholics who couldn't care for themselves. Caring, compassion, and education in a dignified environment were the essence of this new approach to treatment. The grace of a beautiful environment promoted respect, understanding, and acceptance of the dignity of each patient. Treatment was based on the program and process of AA and on the belief that time away and association with other alcoholics were central to recovery.

The first patient to undergo treatment was Patrick Butler's brother Lawrence, who later became one of Hazelden's trustees. Since then over a hundred thousand men and women have gone through treatment in one of Hazelden's facilities. Pat Butler was one of these, having gone to Hazelden in January and then again in July 1950. From that latter date until he died in 1990, he never indulged in another drink.

Treatment was uncomplicated. The simple expectations remained constant: lectures, group sessions, and responsible behavior. For its part, Hazelden provided a beautiful, wholesome, and clean environment, excellent food, and an AA counselor. From the very beginning, however, there was a problem with finances. While the patient census continued to increase slowly over the initial years, it was often very low, and revenues were never enough to cover operating costs.

Richard Coyle Lilly (1884–1959), a prominent banker and financier, had provided the funds for the purchase of Hazelden through the Coyle Foundation. The plan had been that fund-raising would supplement the insufficient fees and take care of other capital expenditures. But the results were rather dismal for 1950. Instead of the $100,000 hoped for by Lilly, only $1,800 was raised, $1,300 of which came from the pockets of Emmett, Lawrence, and Patrick Butler. By 1951 Lilly had had enough and decided to foreclose on the contract for deed on which Hazelden had defaulted. At a special meeting of the board on May 7, 1951, Lilly announced that he had an offer from the Sisters of St. Joseph in Crookston for the property. He gave Hazelden thirty days to come up with the money, and, in a final gesture of generosity, he reduced the payment from $65,000 to $45,000. If Hazelden were unable to raise the money, then the Coyle Foundation, which owned the note, would repossess the property and sell it to the Sisters of St. Joseph. This was the first critical juncture in Hazelden's history.

Pat Butler had been aware of Lilly's reluctance to continue his support. He recalled an unplanned conversation he had had with Lilly early in 1951 after a golf game at the Somerset Country Club in St. Paul. During the course of that talk Lilly had suggested that the Butlers take over Hazelden. He believed that the Sisters of St. Joseph could administer Hazelden in a fiscally responsible fashion, and AA could direct the program. Pat was astute enough to realize that Lilly was making a very attractive proposal.

*P*at wanted Hazelden to feel inviting and humane rather than institutional. He wanted nice facilities that would convey respect and dignity to the alcoholics who came for treatment. That desire translated into a constant flow of ideas for what needed to be done or could be done to improve the place. In fact, Pat always carried a piece of paper in his shirt pocket that had a list of his current ideas. People were often nervous about that list. They'd see Pat and say, "Oh, oh. Here comes Pat with his list." But Pat's response would always be, "Don't worry, these aren't necessarily all good ideas, they're just my ideas. We don't have to do all of them. Let's see how they work out—and if they're no good, they're off the list."

Pat's ideas weren't always followed through on, and as a result, it wasn't unusual for me to hear him complain about "they." He'd say, "Harry, when I ask why something didn't get done, the answer I get is always something like, 'They didn't like the idea,' or, 'They didn't want to do it.' But I can never find out who 'they' is. If you ever find out, please let me know." This was what Pat called the pocket veto.

—HARRY SWIFT

69

The day after the board meeting on May 7, Lawrence Butler, who by this time was a trustee of the board, encouraged by his brother's golfing conversation with Lilly, took Carroll with him to see his father and Patrick. Emmett Butler, who had stopped drinking in 1945, had an obvious interest in Hazelden because of its impact on his sons. While Carroll waited outside Emmett's office, the father and his sons discussed the Hazelden situation and Lilly's generous offer. The thought of getting a bargain from Lilly (Pat observed that Lilly was a "sharp cookie") was an important factor in the discussions. Finally, Lawrence stepped out into the reception area where Carroll was sitting and announced to Hazelden's director, "Well, it's settled. We're taking over." On June 5, 1951, the Coyle Foundation assigned the contract for deed to Emmett, Patrick, and Lawrence Butler. With the Butlers' involvement Hazelden's viability was assured. Their dedication, loyalty, and compassion provided Hazelden with a sense of direction and a spirit of humanity and service, all of which were to evolve into the gracefully nurtured concept of a caring community. Patrick would become president of the board in 1952 and chairman in 1971, a position that he served in until 1989.

With his recovery in 1950, Patrick had very quickly entered into the AA program, attending frequent meetings, and helping other alcoholics. Before the Northwest and Uptown AA clubs were established with his help, Pat occasionally hosted a Sunday morning AA meeting at his home on Summit Avenue. He remodeled the carriage house behind his home and allowed individuals and even families in need to live there. Over the years Pat built up quite an intelligence network to discover those who needed help. Employers, friends, bartenders, wives, and personnel directors knew that they could call upon Pat at any time of the day or night to help an alcoholic or to share the street gossip about who might be on another six-day binge. Pat was always ready to take the initiative, to make the first move to help those in distress.

Beginning in 1951 Pat Butler was asked to speak at Saturday AA meetings at Willmar State Hospital, where the cause of recovery was being actively promoted by Nelson Bradley, the superintendent of the hospital. These meetings had been organized at Bradley's request by Glen Steele, a retired businessman and recovering alcoholic. Speakers were recruited from AA groups statewide: Otto Zapp from St. Cloud; Pat Cronin from "2218" (the Minneapolis AA headquarters at 2218 First Avenue South); Lynn Carroll from Hazelden; Fred Eiden from Hastings State Hospital; Mel Brandes from the Midway AA group in St. Paul; and, as has been mentioned, Pat Butler, who found himself among an eminent group of recovering people from whom he collected ideas and suggestions that could be tested and tried at Hazelden. The lecture series that Hazelden later developed became especially important to him, since educating patients about the nature of the illness was one of the principal goals of Hazelden.

Pat was a very effective speaker—not a great orator, but he could certainly get the AA message across. He understood the importance of helping people break through denial and take Step One. He was very good at telling his story and helping others tell theirs. I believe that part of Pat's reason for being involved in Hazelden was to be able to pass on the AA message, since AA continued to help him so much.

—Dick Frederickson

Pat Butler became more and more involved with the everyday affairs of Hazelden. The treatment center provided him with a sense of purpose and filled a void in his life. His weekly trips to Center City, which started at the time the Butlers took control of Hazelden, allowed him to become intimately and personally aware of the details of the program and its needs. The pilgrimage became an uninterrupted custom for almost forty years, during which he kept a close watch on the interaction between multiple events and people in the evolution of a company. It was an era of benevolent paternalism, in the best sense of the phrase.

When Pat Butler first became involved at Hazelden in the early fifties, he was everywhere and into everything that pertained to alcoholism. Besides his involvement at Willmar and his weekly sojourns to Hazelden, he returned to Yale in 1951 to attend the Summer School of Alcohol Studies. In the coming years he cultivated a close relationship between the summer school (which in 1962 was transferred to Rutgers University) and Hazelden. Butler invited Selden Bacon, the director of the Yale program, and Harry Tiebout, a psychiatrist who was a strong believer that alcoholism was a primary and chronic illness and not a psychiatric disorder, to visit and lecture at Hazelden. Tiebout and Bradley, the superintendent at Willmar, went down to Rochester to address Mayo Clinic doctors, who listened to the presentation on alcoholism respectfully but somewhat condescendingly. In 1953 Butler became vice president of and a director on the National Council on Alcoholism, where he got to know Marty Mann, well known in the field because of her recovery, her gender, and her efforts on behalf of female alcoholics. He invited her to Hazelden, where she spoke to the staff and the patients. She in turn whetted Butler's interest in the plight of women, who had very few places to go for help with their illness.

*P*at had an image of always being in charge, of always wanting this or that done. That image, however, wasn't entirely accurate. Things didn't always have to be Pat's way. He loved a good argument or discussion about what Hazelden should or shouldn't do, and he really listened.

Pat regularly quizzed staff about various projects, and occasionally he'd get what you might call bureaucratic or pseudo answers, ones such as, "It's in the computer," or, "The census is down because the economy is bad."

I learned early on that if Pat asked a question, he usually had a good idea of what the problem was. When he asked me how a particular account was doing, rather than give him the "computer" answer or something along those lines, I'd say, "Pat, that account is screwed up, and I don't know why, but we have time to figure it out." And Pat would reply, "Good, Harry, because I think it's screwed up, too, but nobody's telling me that. Now at least I know someone else is worried about it, too." Pat would then walk away from the problem and not worry about it again; and he'd trust you to do something about it.

—HARRY SWIFT

I met Pat in the early 1950s while I was working at Willmar
State Hospital, trying to establish an alcohol treatment
program there. At this time, Hazelden was not just struggling,
it was going broke. Partly because he wanted to help Hazelden and partly for
his own recovery, Pat was increasing his involvement not only at Hazelden,
but in the broader issues connected with chemical dependency.

One of the major obstacles we faced then was a poor understanding among
policy makers and the general public of alcoholism and treatment. That we
needed to involve ourselves in community education was obvious, so Pat,
Nelson Bradley, then the superintendent at Willmar State Hospital, and I
went on the road quite often to teach. After working all day, we spent
evenings and weekends in church basements, schools, and town halls
throughout the state talking about alcoholism. Pat played the role of an
"industrialist," that is, an employer concerned about alcohol problems among
his employees. Bradley was the physician. I took the role of psychologist, and a
local person from AA was the "AA" representative.

These efforts were truly the beginning of public education about alcoholism
and the idea of employee assistance programs. If you can remember how, in
the mid-1980s, people who spoke about AIDS and the need for help and
treatment for those afflicted were received, you have a good idea about how
we were received. To talk about helping alcoholics was not the least bit
popular, and we ran into some very hostile people and very negative
attitudes. Pat, however, was very good in this role, and played a significant
part in advancing public knowledge about alcohol addiction. . . .

What's important to recognize here is that Pat was, at this time, one of the
few people in the country who had a true public health view of the problem of

alcoholism. Most people who have a chronic illness like alcoholism stay focused on solving the problems it causes in their own lives. It's a rare person who can say, "Wait a minute, I've got this problem, a lot of people in AA have it, and, in fact, there are countless thousands of people all over the country and throughout the world who have this problem. We need to approach it on a far broader level." Pat was a true visionary—a man who could tackle problems on a very personal level and work on them at a society-wide, public-policy level too.

—Dan Anderson

No sooner had the Butlers acquired Hazelden in 1951, than Pat formed a Hazelden advisory council to assist in educating business and industry leaders about the consequences of alcoholism for the workplace and the opportunity that Hazelden offered for recovery. In 1952 he hired Leroy "Bud" Murphy, a friend and recovering alcoholic, to convince the industries in the St. Paul area of the need for a program to help alcoholics—the beginnings of an employee assistance program. Butler's pragmatic mind was at work. He wanted to increase the patient population at Hazelden. "Hazelden had empty beds at that time," Butler noted, "so my effort was not all out of great charity." Because of his activities and reputation, in 1953 he was invited to chair the governor's advisory board on the problems of alcoholism in the State of Minnesota.

The most singular achievements that Pat Butler accomplished in the fifties were his enlargement of Hazelden's continuum of care with the establishment of Fellowship Club (1953) and Dia Linn (1956) and his purchase of the little meditation book entitled *Twenty-Four Hours a Day* (1954).

FELLOWSHIP CLUB

Fellowship Club, the name selected by Patrick Butler, was established in response to a pressing human need—accommodations for men (later it included women) in recovery who were homeless and needed time to adjust to economic and social realities without using alcohol for support. The concept of Fellowship Club developed as a result of Patrick Butler's experiences at Willmar State Hospital, where he spent

Early Fellowship Club, 341 North Dale Street, St. Paul

Fellowship Club, 680 Stewart Avenue, St. Paul

a great deal of time. There, Butler was in constant contact with Nelson Bradley, who, together with Dan Anderson, was a frequent visitor at the Butlers' home in St. Paul. Alcoholics who were treated at Willmar State Hospital would return to their home communities with no job, no place to stay, and no money for the simple necessities of life. Moreover, because of their remote location, these people were often unable to have good linkage with the AA Fellowship. It was clear that some kind of residential aftercare was needed. Hence, the beginning of the halfway house concept.

One day in 1953 Pat Butler was discussing with Hazelden board member George Nienaber and a mutual friend, Father Francis Curtin, the plight of an alcoholic known to the three of them. Despite repeated treatments, he was unable to maintain sobriety. What was needed, the three of them decided, was a halfway house, so that the alcoholic could gradually gather strength and regain a role in society. Father Curtin knew that the Catholic archdiocese had a large vacant building at 341 North Dale Street that had been previously maintained by the Sisters of St. Joseph as a home for infants. It was the right time and the right place. Hazelden purchased and renovated it, and Fellowship Club opened in December 1953.

Fellowship Club ran into a great deal of opposition from residents of the neighborhood, and the St. Paul City Council rejected its petition for licensure. The matter was brought to court, where it was litigated for about a year and then recessed indefinitely in October 1955. Throughout the litigation, Fellowship Club continued to operate and was open to any man who was homeless, penniless, and friendless due to alcoholism. The residents were expected to work at jobs in the community, but in the beginning business owners shied away from hiring alcoholics even though they had been through treatment. Pat went to the College of St. Thomas, where he served on the board, and promised a substantial donation if the university would hire Fellowship Club residents to work part time on the campus maintenance crew. Although initially somewhat hesitant, St. Thomas finally agreed and the venture was successful: the residents proved to be hardworking, conscientious employees. In return, during Father Shannon's presidency at St. Thomas (1956–1966), Pat chaired the university's first major capital fund drive, which turned out to be a great success.

Condemnation proceedings by the Minnesota Department of Highways in 1957 necessitated the search for a new residence, which was found at 680 Stewart Avenue in St. Paul. In October 1958 the residents moved in. An old mansion built in the 1880s from the beer profits of the Bannholzer Van Hoven family, the home stands in clear view of the Schmidt Brewery sign on West Seventh Street in St. Paul—a symbolic reminder of where the residents have been.

Like Hazelden, Fellowship Club followed a simple approach, providing its guests with a clean place to rest and sleep, good and abundant food, lectures, and the opportunity to share with other alcoholics and to internalize the AA principles. The program also strove to reactivate the individual's work ethic and social life without alcohol. Camaraderie, casualness, and liquorless conviviality were hallmarks of Fellowship Club, and people were encouraged to drop in at any time for a cup of coffee.

at and Aimee were regulars at Fellowship Club on Friday nights. I was always so impressed by this. Here was the boss, the chairman of Hazelden's board, sitting through Fellowship Club meetings and participating with the folks who were attending the meetings. I think Pat came to Fellowship Club in part to see how his project was working—and to see if it could be improved.

But more than anything, Pat saw attending Fellowship Club as part of his program. He always took time to introduce himself to the newcomers, though he never made a point of saying exactly who he was or talked about his role at Hazelden.

Pat was generally pretty quiet at the meetings, but he'd pitch in occasionally. When he did, it was in his own unassuming, humble way. I don't know that I ever heard Pat tell someone what to do; rather he would occasionally give someone a suggestion or remind them of one of the AA principles. Pat led by sharing his experiences, not by pontificating or giving instructions. And he led by example. The people who went through Fellowship Club and who knew Pat were all reminded of how to work the program by seeing his faithfulness. Here was a guy who'd been sober for many years and who was still going to meetings.

—Lou Hill

In the mid-1980s, I was an administrator at Hazelden. At some point, another staff member invited me to come to a Friday night open AA meeting at Fellowship Club. At the time, one of my responsibilities was the women's outpatient fellowship program, and I was trying to learn more about what was available in the community. The meeting was a good one, and I remembered seeing Pat there, though I didn't talk to him.

When I got back to work on Monday, however, I received a phone call from Pat. The conversation was actually quite puzzling because I couldn't quite grasp what he really wanted. He was talking about how nice it was to see me at the Fellowship Club meeting that I attended, and he wanted to know if I had any questions about what I'd heard there or anything else. These weren't unusual questions coming from Pat, but still, something felt odd about the conversation.

It wasn't until I hung up, however, that it dawned on me what was going on. Pat knew I wasn't in recovery, and so, after seeing me at Fellowship Club, he had been wondering if I'd gone because I was concerned about my own alcohol use. He was subtly opening the door for help, should I need it. What's more, he did it in such a way that if I had had a problem, I would have opened up to him immediately, without question. I was so floored and so touched that this man would do this. It was just so very thoughtful.

What made Pat so remarkable was how thoughtful, unpretentious, and unassuming he was. Some people in leadership positions blow their own horns, but Pat was the opposite. He didn't need to announce anything. He just acted, and then let those actions speak for themselves.

—PAT OWEN

Butler visited Fellowship Club often and helped the men realize just what was meant by the spirituality of the program and by the expression "But for the grace of God." He also provided impromptu lectures on golfing and smoking, often remarking that Walter Hagen, the famous golfer, never chain-smoked. By that time Pat had kicked his own smoking habit.

DIA LINN

In 1956 the Minnesota Advisory Board on the Problems of Alcoholism, chaired by Pat Butler, believed the help available for female alcoholics was grossly inadequate. Consequently, the board recommended that the Minnesota state legislature establish a commission to look into the problem and report its findings to the 1957 legislature. Rather than wait for the commission's findings, Butler and other Hazelden board members committed themselves to doing something on their own. They decided to create a facility where the primary disease of alcoholism would be dealt with in an environment responsive to the needs and the dignity of women.

Butler had been unsuccessful in persuading Lynn Carroll to set aside some acres of Hazelden's Center City campus for a women's treatment unit. "They did not make bear traps big enough to keep them [men and women] apart," Carroll was reported to have said. Butler decided to look elsewhere.

He began his search for a suitable location in Minneapolis, where his endeavors were blocked by zoning and fire regulations. In St. Paul, neighbors had already complained about the existence and location of Fellowship Club. A similar reaction to a treatment facility for women was heard from Stillwater residents. Butler, again with the help of George Nienaber, finally found a more isolated location in Dellwood, near White Bear Lake, outside the Twin Cities.

The grounds and the facilities had been the home of W. O. Washburn, a St. Paul industrialist, and had been operated as a gentleman's farm. The setting was ideal for the dignified treatment of alcoholism. In addition to the main manor, there were a small guest cottage and two other cottages all in excellent condition and ready for year-round occupancy. Able to house about twelve women, the facility opened in July 1956.

Butler, upon returning from a trip to Ireland, christened the facility *Dia Linn*, Gaelic for "God be with us," a phrase expressing polite concern for the status of another person's health. The new patients' nightmarish expectations of treatment were quickly dispelled by the soft beauty of the tall pines, the circular driveway, the fragrant flower gardens, and the beautiful mansion and cottages. There were no bars on the windows, no dungeon lock or bolts. Whatever apprehension lingered gradually disappeared when the newly arrived guests were shown the interior of the facilities: the cozy furnishings, the fireplace, the easy chairs, the television room, and the beautiful view from the bedroom windows—especially the view of the rose garden.

Nearly everyone who visited Dia Linn during the spring or summer months remarked on the rose garden, described by the *Dia Linn Newsletter* as "the most beautiful rose garden in the world." The rose garden symbolized everything Dia Linn stood for—the promise of recovery and the delicacy, dignity, and potential growth of the recovering woman. Pat Butler's remarkable sensitivity to the needs of the alcoholic, reinforced by the personal experience of his own recovery and his wife's illness, enabled him to respond creatively to the personal dignity of those seeking help.

BEGINNINGS OF PUBLISHING AT HAZELDEN

It would take some time before the significance of Butler's third contribution during the decade of the fifties—Hazelden's modest beginnings in the field of publications—was understood by others. In 1952 Butler came across a small volume entitled *Twenty-Four Hours a Day,* a meditation book for recovering alcoholics. The author, Richmond Walker of Daytona Beach, Florida, was publishing, selling, and distributing the volume himself. Butler offered to assume the publication and distribution of the work. Walker agreed, after the General Service Board of AA showed no interest in the undertaking. Consequently, in May 1954, Hazelden purchased the rights to *Twenty-Four Hours a Day.* Nearly five thousand copies were sold the first year, and the book still enjoys an immense popularity. Composed of a short thought, a brief meditation, and a prayer for each day of the year, the book serves as a spiritual uplift for legions of readers. As Pat Butler himself recalled

> I did not realize the high esteem the little book has assumed in the minds of people until I went to a wake. In a Catholic wake, quite often you will see entwined in the hands of the deceased a rosary or a prayer book therein. In this particular case, I was startled to see the *Twenty-Four Hours a Day* book in his hands. So you are able to see in what high esteem a great many people

The origin of Hazelden's publishing venture began in 1954 when Pat Butler purchased the rights to publish Twenty-Four Hours a Day, *a daily meditation book whose format is immensely popular even today.*

held that book. And it's been a great aid to a great many people—particularly a lot of loners all over the world.

This little book became the model for the meditation books that Hazelden was so successful in publishing in the eighties and that were then copied by other publishers throughout the world.

Chapter 7

FAMILY LIFE AND SHOW HORSES

While Pat Butler spent a great deal of his time and energy at Hazelden and helping alcoholics during the fifties, it was not his only love and outlet. Love and attention also went to his family. In 1955 Butler's father died at the age of eighty-five. Emmett Butler had been a powerful figure in the construction and mining industries. In the mining operations he had continued the spirit of ingenuity and innovation that Butler Brothers had begun in the construction business. Upon Emmett's death, a business associate and the former head of the University of Minnesota's Mines Experimental Station commented, "Practically every new technique which has proven of value to the mining industry in the past twenty-five years has been brought about by Emmett Butler. With Emmett in charge, the company gained a national reputation. He faced the new, the untried with a welcome and daring that are given to few men." At the time of his death, Emmett was negotiating to bring natural gas to the Minnesota Iron Range.

A few years after his father's death, Pat Butler's mother was hospitalized, where she remained in a private suite at United Hospital for five years until she died in 1963. There was not one morning that Butler did not visit her unless he was out of town. He had a deep and abiding love for his parents. He transferred this love to the extended Butler family as he gradually assumed the role during his recovery of the beloved and trusted patriarch, to whom the rest were easily drawn because of his compassion, sensitivity, and wisdom.

Butler's wife, Aimee, suffered through a long period of depression during the fifties. Sons Patrick and Peter were away at college from 1949 until 1953, Patrick graduating from Harvard and Peter from Yale. Both were married in 1958, Patrick to Patricia Catherine Maynard, and Peter to Mary Sandra Kamman. The sons were not in St. Paul often during these years of their mother's illness. Kate would have been very much alone had not her father encouraged and allowed nieces and nephews to live with them. Cooley's daughter, Cean, who was the same age as Kate, spent most of her high school years there and was a welcome companion for Kate.

Another diversion for Kate was her interest in horses. In fact, she was instrumental in kindling her parents' interest in thoroughbred horse jumpers. Pat Butler recalled, "It all started when I took her to one of those places—Eaton's, I think—where you pay $2 to ride a horse." The year was 1950. Kate was ten years old, and Pat had just started his recovery. From that first ride, Kate fell in love with horses. Pat bought Kate a horse and, when she was ready, introduced her to the local show circuit. At the age of twelve Kate was entering horse shows in the Midwest, and her parents began purchasing first-class jumping horses for their daughter. At the Minnesota State Horse Show, Kate became the jumper champion in 1967 and the hunter champion in 1968.

Back in 1961 the Butlers had learned from the coach of the United

States Equestrian Team (USET), Bertalan de Nemethy, of the team's need for good horses. The Butlers agreed to make their horses available to the team and began purchasing first-class jumpers for the national and international horse show circuit. The Butlers did not have their own stable and did not raise their own horses. When they began the venture, they boarded the horses in St. Paul, but eventually the horses summered in Southampton, on Long Island in New York, and wintered in West Palm Beach, Florida. The Butlers lent some of the finest jumpers in the world to the United States Equestrian Team.

In addition to supporting the USET in the Olympics, the Butlers also sponsored individual riders, including Kathy Kusner, who eventually became one of the top riders in the world. She was primarily instrumental in popularizing show jumping with the American public. For five years the Butlers sent Kusner abroad with their horses, helping to bridge the gap between the growth of open jumping in the United States and the well-established and popular sport of show jumping in Europe. During that time Kusner rode only Butler horses. In 1965 she won twelve events in Europe and the United States on Butler mounts, most of them riding Untouchable, one of the Butlers' most famous horses. Kusner also rode Untouchable in the 1964 and 1968 Olympics held in Mexico City and Tokyo, respectively. In 1972 the Butlers' horse Sloopy, ridden by Neal Shapiro, won the bronze medal at the Olympics in Munich. Conrad Homfeld, riding Balbuco, another of the Butler horses, was the first American to win the World Cup Championship in 1980. Balbuco was the horse of the year in both 1979 and 1980. Touch of Class (ridden by Joe Fargis) won the gold medal in the 1984 Olympics and was number thirty in a long line of horses owned by the Butlers. According to Aimee, the win left

The Butlers, who, through their daughter, Kate, developed a keen interest in thoroughbred horse jumpers, sponsored Kathy Kusner, pictured here on Untouchable, one of the Butlers' most famous horses. Kusner became one of the world's top riders.

Pat speechless for five minutes. When he was able to talk, he called Aimee and said that perhaps they had better buy another horse even though they had decided against further purchases.

Less well known than the Butler horses but equally important was Pat Butler's solicitude at horse shows for those who had alcohol and drug problems, a solicitude and compassion instrumental in helping some of them recover their sobriety. Pat once remarked in a sober but humorous fashion, "I spend a good deal of time at horse shows proselytizing."

Pat thought that horses, unlike alcohol, were a hobby worth getting addicted to. The interest also helped Aimee overcome her years of depression. She enjoyed her travels with Pat around the United States and Europe to attend many of the events that their horses were participating in. It was clearly the joy of the sport that maintained the Butlers' interest in horse show competition. The winning purses were minimal compared with the expenses of purchasing, maintaining, and transporting a top show horse. The cups and ribbons from their horses were spread casually throughout their apartment on River Drive. Pat noted, "I wouldn't have any fun just owning horses. I have to be there to watch them in action. That's the big thrill. I have to be involved with the entire activity."

at was very interested in horses and horse racing, a hobby that took him all over the world. During his travels, Pat ran across people in the horse business—jockeys, veterinarians, stablehands, owners, and so on— who were chemically dependent. And with regularity, he'd manage to get some of them to come to Hazelden for help.

We used to call these people Pat's recruits. Pat's horses used to set records, and so did his "recruits." Some of the longest lengths of stay in extended care were made by his horse show recruits. Many were in dire need of long-term care, and some of the people he brought into the Family Program had some of the most complex problems we'd ever seen.

Every time Pat was gone, staff would wonder whom he'd be bringing back. We used to joke about it, wondering why he couldn't just find these people sooner so they wouldn't be so bad off by the time they got here.

It was truly remarkable, actually, that Pat was able to persuade so many people who were so sick to even come in for treatment. But Pat was always a master of the soft sell.

— HARRY SWIFT

Chapter 8

Irish Heritage, Catholic Faith

From the day Pat Butler was born, pride in his Irish roots coursed through his blood. Ireland was another area of interest where he would make a quiet but remarkable contribution. It all came about in 1960, when a man by the name of Eoin McKiernan was driving through Dellwood and saw the sign outside Hazelden's treatment center for women that read Dia Linn. He thought it remarkable that this Gaelic blessing should be found in Minnesota. A second-generation Irishman born and raised in New York City, deeply imbedded in Irish culture and history, McKiernan felt compelled to find out more about this strange Irish apparition in Scandinavian Minnesota. His search led him to a meeting with Pat Butler. They discovered they had something in common—their Irish background and their love of Irish culture. McKiernan saw that Butler had very deep feelings for Ireland and knew a great deal about it. He read and respected authors like Yeats and Joyce. In 1962 Minnesota Public Television offered to produce a show on Ireland narrated by McKiernan (who at the time chaired the English Literature Department at the College of St. Thomas) if

McKiernan could find a sponsor. Pat Butler agreed to fund the program. The series lasted for thirteen weeks and was so successful that another series of forty weeks was broadcast nationally in 1963. Butler funded that also.

During the time of these television shows, Butler and McKiernan were assessing the potential for an institute that would raise the consciousness of Irish culture in the United States. Butler always shrewdly elicited enough information to determine whether an idea would last, and he decided that this would be a worthwhile venture. In 1962 Pat Butler and McKiernan cofounded the Irish American Cultural Institute. The goals of the institute were to increase the awareness of Irish history and culture in the United States and to provide assistance for the arts in Ireland. The publicity that Irish life and history gained from the public television series enhanced the growth of the Irish American Cultural Institute. With his very strong interest in the history, literature, and architecture of Ireland, Butler was an active director and participant at the institute's board meetings until he died, and McKiernan served as the institute's president until 1986.

The institute explores and promotes the richness and diversity of Irish culture in a number of ways. It has members and chapters nationwide, and it also fosters a variety of programs, including a summer study and travel seminar for high school students, a nationwide lecture and performance series, grants and awards for writers and artists in Ireland, a research fund for scholars exploring the history of Irish Americans, and the publication of *Eire-Ireland*, a multidisciplinary journal of Irish studies. Butler was especially active in supporting literature. Beginning in 1966, he sponsored the institute's first annual arts award, now called the Butler Literary Award, which in alternating years honors writers in English and in the Irish language. In 1986 Butler established a permanent endowment to fund this award. At the first Irish American Cultural Institute awards dinner in 1975, Princess Grace of Monaco presented to Aimee and Patrick Butler a medallion designed by a Northern Ireland artist for the Butlers' substantial contributions to Irish culture.

Part of Pat Butler's Irish heritage involved Catholicism. Butler's love of the Church and his interest in things Catholic prompted many undertakings. He was a founder and charter member of the Calix Society (an AA group for Catholics). He was an active participant of the Serra Club, founded to promote and finance vocations to the priesthood. He was elected to the boards at St. Thomas and the College of St. Catherine and was a generous contributor to both. It was probably because St. Thomas had been receptive to his request for part-time jobs for Fellowship Club clients that Butler served as general chairman of the Program for Great Teaching, a three-year solicitation effort (1962–1965) that brought the college gifts totaling more than $6 million.

Less known is his relationship with the Institute for Ecumenical and Cultural Research at St. John's Abbey and University in Collegeville, Minnesota. It began in 1960, when Butler provided a grant for Father Kilian McDonnell, a monk at St. John's, to go to Europe for graduate studies in Protestant theology. When McDonnell returned to Minnesota, Butler asked him, "Where do we go from here?" McDonnell's response was his vision for a residential research institute that would link the new ecumenical openness of the Church with the long tradition of scholarship among

Benedictine monks. Butler agreed to provide McDonnell's estimated cost of $250,000. Later, embarrassed because he had underestimated the costs of subsidizing scholars and their families, McDonnell had to ask for another $100,000. Butler, understanding the poor fiscal training of the clergy, did not deny the request.

In 1968, three years after the Second Vatican Council introduced so many changes into the Catholic Church, Butler became one of the founding members of McDonnell's Institute for Ecumenical and Cultural Research, which promotes research, discussion, and prayer about what it means to be a Christian in the modern world. Since its initiation, the institute has been recognized for the outstanding service it has provided in advancing dialogue among Christians of all denominations. Perhaps with foreknowledge and understanding of the role Butler would take in this effort, in 1963 John XXIII, the Ecumenical Pope, inducted Pat Butler into the Knights of St. Gregory for his contributions to the Catholic Church.

ometime in 1966, not long after I first started working at Hazelden and not long after the new treatment unit opened, Pat hosted a party for the entire staff—which then was only about thirty people.

I remember being a bit nervous beforehand, and I felt that I needed to get dressed up for this party. Most of us in AA at that time weren't wealthy; in fact, most of us had lost just about everything, financially and otherwise. We were lucky to even have a suit, let alone a nice one.

All of us had gathered in the dining room before the meal. While I was talking to Pat, he moved a bit—and about $1.50 in change rolled out on the floor next to him. Apparently, Pat had a hole in his pants pocket, and the money had fallen down his pants leg onto the floor.

Needless to say, all of us, including Pat, had a good laugh. We all knew that if anyone could afford a new coat and pants, it was Pat—but the sport coat and pants he had on looked like they hadn't been pressed in a good while. Pat was never out to impress anyone, and though he was always presentable, he never flaunted his wealth.

Pat did give a lot of money to Hazelden as well as to other organizations. I think he saw this as a way he could help a great many people. Pat was a very good and very simple man—in the best sense of the word. In a lot of little ways that few people ever saw, Pat contributed more than any of us realized to individuals and to AA.

—DICK F.

eople who've been associated with Hazelden over the years are well aware of the enormous contributions Pat Butler made to that organization. The reach of Pat's generosity, however, extended beyond Hazelden.

As Hazelden's first chaplain many years ago, I directed the Clinical Pastoral Education Program, through which we trained clergy to work with alcoholics. Dan Anderson, Harry Swift, and I had come to a point at which we wanted to expand the program by giving someone a stipend to cover expenses for a full year of training.

One day Pat stopped by, and during a breakfast discussion of the matter, Pat suggested that their [Pat and Aimee Butler's] foundation could be a source for the money.

I was working full time at Hazelden, but Lutheran Social Services was paying half my salary with Hazelden picking up the remainder. In part for this reason, Pat, Dan, and I met in Minneapolis with Dr. Luthard Gjerde, who was then the head of Lutheran Social Services. We talked about increasing our budget by $25,000 or $30,000 as a place to start.

Then Dr. Gjerde's phone rang, and it was for Pat. After quite a time on the phone, Pat came back to the table and sat down. He looked at me and said, "Well, I'm sorry, Gordy. I think we'll just have to take the money for the Clinical Pastoral Education Program out of Hazelden's budget because Aimee and I just gave $250,000 to help Lutheran General Hospital get their alcoholism treatment program started." The Butlers also had a strong interest in the Institute for Ecumenical and Cultural Research at St. John's University in Collegeville, and they gave substantial gifts to the institute over the years. Pat's son Peter continues to keep both these interests alive; he is a member of both the Hazelden Board of Trustees and a member of the Ecumenical Center Council.

—GORDON GRIMM

Chapter 9

Expansion at Hazelden

In 1965, while the Ecumenical Institute and the Irish American Cultural Institute were getting started and the Butler horses were winning an astounding number of events, Hazelden was also experiencing good fortune. That was the year that Hazelden expanded from the Old Lodge into the multifacility complex that visitors see today. The buildings symbolize Pat Butler's greatest achievement—merging the various components of what would become known as the Minnesota Model.

Because of Pat Butler, some of Minnesota's practitioners who treated alcoholics in the fifties had been sharing their experiences with scholars from the Yale Summer School of Alcohol Studies. There was a sense and spirit of being at the edge of a new frontier in helping a major group of the helpless. Pat Butler was a central piece in the convergence of these fascinating events. Nelson Bradley, the superintendent at Willmar State Hospital, recalled, "My life ended up [being spent] between Willmar and Summit Avenue." By Summit Avenue, he meant the St. Paul residence of Patrick Butler, where he spent a great deal of time visiting and sharing experiences with treatment methods.

A walking trail cuts through a wooded area on the Hazelden grounds.

Even today, as described in 1955, "the Hazelden grounds are a spot of heaven. It is really most beautiful with the green grass, shrubs, and flowers." Both Pat and Aimee Butler were primarily responsible for the beauty of the Hazelden grounds, which continue to symbolize what people can do with their lives if they try.

Lush foliage and the resplendent garden area in back of the Renewal Center

Hazelden created an environment that removed the institutional aspects associated with a hospital, especially one treating the mentally ill. From the beginning Hazelden resonated with the belief in the dignity of the alcoholic—in what made an alcoholic a human being, possessing worth and deserving of respect. Recognizing the dignity of the alcoholic came naturally to Hazelden; it was not the result of bureaucratic licensure. Everything was done to provide comfort, cleanliness, and a caring ambiance, whether it be interior decorating, landscaping, or recreational opportunities. Hazelden could always be, for anyone who wanted it to be, a home away from home.

Hazelden was not an institution like Willmar. It was a small, home-like manor that provided an atmosphere for rest, reflection, and personal reinforcement. The grounds, where wildlife flourished, were kept in excellent condition. In 1955 the *Hazelden Newsletter* recorded that "the Hazelden grounds are a spot of heaven. It is really most beautiful with the green grass, shrubs, and flowers. . . . It is our plan to continuously improve the appearance and usefulness of Hazelden since it is symbolic of what men can do with their lives if they but try." Flower boxes on the terrace, forty thousand newly planted fir trees, turtles in the patio pool, purple birdhouses for martins, a shuffleboard and a horseshoe court, the smell of home cooking, fresh paint and varnish—all contributed to an environment conducive to the restoration of the alcoholic's dignity and sense of self-worth. Pat Butler was principally responsible for the maintenance and the continual growth of this environment.

I think that too often people only see the Butlers' major contributions, primarily, I suppose, because they're so obvious. But Pat was effective at many levels—from the corporate and public-policy arenas to the individual. I remember well a time when I was able to convince a fellow I knew to go into treatment at Hazelden. Some time later, I ran into Pat, who asked me how so-and-so was doing. Apparently Pat had reviewed the patient list, which indicated who'd referred the man, and he just wanted to follow up—not to be intrusive, but just because he cared so much about people.

—FRED LAUERMAN

LESSONS FROM WILLMAR

Butler was well aware of what was happening at Willmar. He entertained Bradley and his disciple, a young psychologist named Dan Anderson, at his home. From the discussions that he held with them, Butler discovered the wonderful things that were going on at Willmar. Both literally and figuratively, Bradley unlocked the doors for the alcoholics at Willmar. He separated them from the mentally ill. He established a program for them that relied heavily upon lectures. He hired recovering alcoholics and revealed to Butler that there was a movement at the hospital for all the professional staff to meet and to work together—a miraculous accomplishment—to help the alcoholic. Gradually, things began to converge. The professionals surrendered their superfluous perquisites and exaggerated professionalism for the common team professionalism of assisting the alcoholic client. The team found itself sharing patients. The jealousy and turf associated with "my patient" were abandoned in the common dispensation of care. As the Reverend John Keller, who was sent by the Lutheran Church to train at the hospital recollected, "I'd sit in a staff meeting at Willmar and see a recovering alcoholic disagree with a physician, but then they'd walk out and still be friends. It did not break their relationship. People were here to be together and bring their individual and collective knowledge and experience to provide the care the patients needed."

Pat's vision and energy pushed Hazelden to broaden its reach, too. Hazelden started out as a small, very AA-oriented institution quite unwilling to approach the problem of alcoholism from any other perspective. Once Pat came along, he encouraged me to come to Hazelden to work and to introduce the Willmar treatment model. I did so, and not long after I started, Pat came to me and asked me if Hazelden should have a counselor training program along the lines of the one we had developed at Willmar. I told him that, yes, we could do such a program, but that we'd always lose money doing it. You don't need a formal training program if you're just training your own people.

Pat responded by asking, "But Dan, do we need it?" He was really asking whether such a program was needed beyond Hazelden—does society need it. Clearly there was a tremendous need for more well-trained counselors, so of course I said yes—and Pat's reply was, "Well, let's do it."

After starting Hazelden's counselor training program, our next step was to recruit Gordy Grimm, who had developed a clinical pastoral education program at Willmar State Hospital, to help us develop a similar program for clergy at Hazelden. Today, Hazelden graduates of these programs work and teach all over the world—all because of Pat's vision. That's public health. Pat's vision and commitment really helped push Hazelden to be forward-looking and strive to be a pioneer in the field, something that's easy to forget when an organization grows and ages.

—DAN ANDERSON

By 1959 Willmar State Hospital had an informal multidisciplinary team (although each discipline was still trying to find its own niche and define its own peculiar role) and had installed a formal counselor training program, a formal pastoral training program, and a modest research department. By the time Bradley left to take another position at Lutheran General Hospital in Chicago in 1960, the hospital had adopted a multidisciplinary approach to alcoholism and treated it both as a disease and as a primary problem. For Bradley the fifties had been an adventure. He particularly remembered the support that he had received from Pat Butler during his visits to Summit Avenue. The spirit of that Willmar adventure was to cascade like a mighty cataract into Hazelden during the sixties, inspiring what was to become the refined and finely calibrated Minnesota Model. During the long evenings and equally long conversations with Bradley and the young Dan Anderson, Butler knew intuitively that he would have to import to the Hazelden setting the essential aspects of the Willmar program, the most important of which was the multidisciplinary concept.

THE GREAT BRIDGE BUILDER

Regarding the Minnesota experience, Butler can be thought of as the *Pontifex Maximus,* which in the days of Imperial Rome meant the "high priest," or, literally translated from the Latin, "the great bridge builder" in the sense of connecting Hazelden and Willmar. Butler's primary focus during the fifties was recovery and how to make Hazelden the best rehabilitation center possible. But he was very aware of Bradley's innovative style and was excited about events at Willmar. He saw great possibilities in linking the private, freestanding Hazelden to the discoveries and the direction of Willmar State Hospital. As the *Pontifex Maximus,* he forged the treatment links between Willmar and Hazelden. He made Hazelden the inspiration for dignified treatment and the beneficiary of the hospital's expertise and its multidisciplinary approach.

A keen observer of people, Butler soon intuited the potential of the young Dan Anderson. He gradually came to believe that Anderson had the capability of spanning the geographical distance and attitudinal differences between Willmar and Center City. In 1953, during a dinner conversation that he had at his home on Summit Avenue with Bradley and Anderson, Butler offered to finance their educations if they would assist in forging the future of the Hazelden venture. Through Butler's munificence, Anderson's talents and vision were subsequently tied to Center City. After he finished his doctoral work at the University of Ottawa, Canada, in 1957, and returned to Willmar State Hospital, Anderson began to consult at Hazelden every other Saturday, delivering lectures and providing psychological testing through the Minnesota Multiphasic Personality Inventory (MMPI). The patients, including women transported from Dia Linn, enjoyed his lectures. They particularly liked hearing the MMPI results, which Anderson personally shared with them.

The staff, however, was not all that pleased with the arrival of the psychologist. Lynn Carroll, especially, had some strong views about this. In his eyes, Anderson represented psychology and the Yale Summer School of Alcohol Studies, both of which he felt challenged the purity of the AA approach to recovery. Carroll noted Yale's

Dan Anderson

Pat Butler rightly believed that Anderson could bring the multidisciplinary approach that succeeded at Willmar to Hazelden.

intellectual research into the problem of alcoholism ran counter to Bill W.'s letting go, that is, his abdication of his sovereign, inquiring intellect in the matter of recovery. On one occasion when Carroll's assistant, Lon Jacobson, said that he might like to go to the Yale summer school, Carroll barked at him, "What the hell do you want to go there for? You know more than all those Easterners."

But Butler was in charge. In 1961, the year after Bradley went to Lutheran General Hospital in Chicago, Dan Anderson accepted Butler's offer to become executive director and vice president of Hazelden. With Anderson came the ideas and methods that had been tried and tested at Willmar State Hospital—a detoxification program, a primary care program, a combined aftercare and outpatient program, and, especially, a multidisciplinary response to a multiphasic disease. Both Hazelden and Willmar shared the same philosophy—the disease concept of alcoholism and the AA program for recovery. Anderson's appointment would be the source of conflict between Butler and Carroll and between Carroll and Anderson. But Butler had built the bridge and no one was going to undermine it.

AN EXPANDING PATIENT CENSUS

In the early sixties Hazelden was experiencing a serious, but not unwelcome, problem—an influx of patients that taxed the creative energies of the staff to find space for them. Between 1958 and 1964 the patient population doubled. Every available space was taken. The staff, often upon returning from an overnight stay away from Center City, could never be sure if their beds would be taken.

*T*here was an enormous debate over expanding Hazelden in the mid-sixties, and many were dead set against it, thinking it would destroy the organization. More than a few staff thought Pat was out of his mind for wanting to do it. This was a very traumatic time, but he felt expansion was the right thing to do, and he went ahead with it.

Soon after the expansion was complete, a young African American was admitted for treatment at the Hazelden–Center City facility. When this happened, a number of patients were very upset—so upset, in fact, that they threatened to leave Hazelden if she stayed. The response of Pat and others was to say, "Well, we're sorry about that, but if they feel they have to leave, then that's what they have to do. But this person stays." Pat's statement was quiet and matter-of-fact—and without rancor. I might add, too, that his decision was made at a time when the treatment buildings were quite new and we had a lot of empty beds. To take the chance that a number of paying patients would leave was no small matter.

—HARRY SWIFT

On the day after Christmas, 1963, Pat Butler talked with the staff about the alternatives that the board had considered for expansion and indicated that a great deal of thought had been given to choosing a location outside of Minnesota, particularly in the Chicago/Milwaukee axis because of the large number of referrals from that locale. The decision had been made, however, to remain in Center City with its core staff and to add new units as needed rather than to start an entirely new operation in another city and state.

There had been a great deal of agonizing over this decision. Bringing men and women together on the same campus was opposed by a good number of board members, staff, and alumni. Indeed, larger numbers demanded new buildings. But would more and larger buildings eventually mean fewer numbers? Would the initial increase in numbers destroy whatever was in the "little black box," the secret formula for success that made treatment at the Old Lodge so successful? It was not only patients who could get into "awfulizing," or seeing the worst in everything. Suppose Hazelden doubled and even tripled its capacity and no one were to come. Suppose the program were to be modified and it were no longer effective? Whatever it was at the Old Lodge—the small size, the familiarity, the intimacy, the freedom, the simplicity—it worked. People came, people were restored, people departed, people recovered—it was a simple enough formula. Would institutionalizing Hazelden destroy it?

*P**at and Hazelden staff also had to work through another issue, one that was less critical than admitting and treating drug addicts, but nonetheless very emotional— whether or not to tear down the Old Lodge, Hazelden's original building. At the time of this discussion, the Old Lodge was essentially unusable and irreparable. A few years before this, the fire marshal had warned us that if we continued to have patients in the building, we'd be in big trouble. We then converted it to staff use, but that was a poor solution, too—the staff disliked the building since the heat didn't work well, nor did the water. Bats lived in the attic, and it was a fire hazard.*

The alumni, however, loved the Old Lodge, even though they rarely visited the building when they were on campus. We'd reached the point where it had to go, but no one wanted to make the decision. Even the board of trustees was divided over the question.

One day Pat finally spoke out at a board meeting. He said, "Okay, I'll stand up and claim the privilege of being the only person in this room who was a patient in that building, so this gives me the right to speak from some authority." Then he told this story:

"The Old Lodge reminds me of the time when the boys had left the farm and moved to the city to make their fortunes. Their mother kept the farm. Finally, it came time to do something with the farm, so she got the boys together and said, 'What should I do with the farm? Sell it?' And the boys said, 'No, mother, just give the damn thing away. Please!' And that's the way I feel about the Old Lodge. Let's give it away."

Pat had perhaps the strongest sentimental attachment to that building, but he was also able to make the decision and say that its time had passed and it had to go.

—Harry Swift

120

Numbers and effectiveness—these were the issues. Hazelden was at a crossroads. The decision to expand was a risk involving also a large financial outlay that would have to be undertaken by the Butlers. To secure the bank loan, Aimee Butler's trust fund was used as collateral. The Butlers felt that it was worth the risk, for the expansion meant providing, in the words of Pat Butler, "the best help at the least cost to as many alcoholics as possible." This was Pat Butler's mission and it was to prevail as Hazelden's corporate culture.

CONSTRUCTION OF NEW UNITS

Aimee and Pat Butler took a special interest in the new buildings, and they included Dan Anderson in their conferences with the architects from Voight and Fourré, the St. Paul architectural firm that was hired for the task. The architects were continually reminded of the board's concern about Hazelden becoming too large, too impersonal, and too institutionalized. They were urged to keep in mind that the success of the program was in its small numbers and casual atmosphere. In addition, the architects needed to keep in mind the conflicting demands inherent in treating the many aspects of alcoholism, an illness with physical, mental, and spiritual components. They were told that although the alcoholic was sometimes very ill physically for a short period of time, a hospital setting was not envisioned; although many alcoholics were emotionally upset, a mental hospital was not wanted; and, while many required spiritual help, there was no need for a church. It was further explained that the atmosphere should combine that of a motel, a hotel, and a residential club, but with a

In response to the board's concern that Hazelden become too impersonal and institutionalized, the architects who designed Hazelden's new buildings envisioned a "therapeutic community," a "hill village" — "a neighborhood within the total community."

difference left to the ingenuity of the architects. The total conception was that of a therapeutic community in which individuals could be exposed to small groups of other patients. The architects faced a formidable challenge to create something unique, unprecedented, and unparalleled in the history of caregiving.

Under the watchful eyes of the Butlers and Anderson, the architects' solution was to provide a small and intimate unit atmosphere while making the individual part of the larger community of Hazelden during lectures and meals. They conceived the whole complex as a sort of "hill village" and described the process in a simple fashion: "Each residence building, of eighteen to twenty-two beds, comprises a basic therapeutic unit, having an 'integral form' and becomes a 'neighborhood within the total community.' The result is a cohesive architectural design that has form in itself and also gives form to the program it shelters." Ground was broken by the Butlers on a rainy Saturday in August 1964. Two units were ready for occupancy by January 1966, the other two in April of the same year. Despite the additions, two years later there was a need for more beds. The Butlers could be proud of their buildings and the success of their programs.

In 1979, at the age of thirty-two, and after four months of treatment at Hazelden, I moved to Fellowship Club. To help residents adjust to everyday life and to learn responsibility, Fellowship Club staff helped residents find jobs. The one I received was to vacuum hallway floors in the high-rise apartment building in which the Butlers lived.

One day while I was vacuuming, Pat came out into the hall and introduced himself. I, of course, had no idea who he was, and thought he was just an older guy trying to be friendly. As time went on, we found ourselves talking fairly often while I was working. Pat learned that I was recovering, and, at one point, he told me he wanted to be my AA sponsor—which he was from 1980 until his death. Here was a very wealthy, very influential man who was so down-to-earth and still willing to take the time to sponsor a newcomer—"to pass it on," as we say.

—BILL P.

Today, a visitor's immediate impressions of Hazelden are warmth, light, space, color, cleanliness, and coziness. This atmosphere is created not only by the architectural design but also by the artwork that graces the walls. It was Pat's idea that Aimee find some pictures to hang on Hazelden's bare walls. His request initiated her lifelong interest in Minnesota artists and art. A Hazelden publication entitled *Visions and Hope* noted, "In building the Hazelden art collection Aimee not only accepted the works of regional artists, but championed them and made them available for others to appreciate." She not only found paintings but selected colors and materials for many of the buildings. Like her husband, Aimee eventually began to visit Hazelden one day a week, when she met with members of the staff and created the Butler Art Crew, whose button she often wore with amusement and probably pride. Her art collections humanized the halls of Hazelden, offering a sense of hope to the patients passing through the corridors. The warm colors of still lifes and landscapes helped emphasize the humane and respectful environment so vital to the Minnesota Model of treatment developed at Hazelden.

A CHANGING OF THE GUARD

The winds of change exemplified by the addition of the new buildings were also to bring about a changing of the guard—old departures and new arrivals. The years 1963 to 1966 were difficult from the point of view of personal transitions and change, particularly for Carroll and Anderson. With the expansion, Anderson moved his office to Center City and began a series of planning meetings in anticipation of the opening of the new units. Carroll attended initially but his participation was perfunctory. In January 1965 Anderson began to hire a variety of professionals to assist in the multidisciplinary model, some of whom, as was to be expected, were psychologists.

Since 1965 Carroll had resumed his journeys through the Midwest and into Canada, reverting to his role in the forties and fifties as a missionary, preaching the message of AA. But he was no longer carrying the message under the sponsorship of Hazelden, and his disenchantment with the direction that Hazelden was taking and with the professional staff that it was hiring crept into his talks, sometimes subtly, sometimes not. Carroll had a great following and there was serious question as to whether his public disillusionment with the way things were going at Hazelden would affect the number of patient admissions.

Carroll had been Pat Butler's sponsor, so it was particularly difficult for Pat to reprimand Carroll for the harm he was causing and finally to ask him to leave the campus. For fifteen years Carroll had provided the foundation and the development of a rehabilitation process based substantially upon AA, set in a dignified, warm, humane, and personally enriching environment. Anderson was welding that program with his own tradition, again based substantially upon AA, but systematically and structurally delivered through a multidisciplinary method. Of course, there were major and minor differences, depending on the viewpoint of the old or the new guard. The old guard saw them as major. As a consequence, Butler felt that it was time for a changing of the guard.

In a manner of speaking, Butler passed the baton to Anderson and gave him the freedom to be as creative as he wanted. As a result, the period from 1966 to 1976 was one of the most innovative and expansive in Hazelden's history. It was a time of amazing vitality, marked by a relentless flow of ideas and endless experimentation. The events that occurred during this time were guided by a group of dedicated, strong-willed individuals, diverse in tradition, character, and personality, who molded Hazelden for years to come. With the support and encouragement of Butler, these years witnessed (1) the solidification of a clearly defined treatment program with a multidisciplinary approach; (2) the creation of a short-lived repeaters program that became the model for relapse programs around the country; (3) the establishment of an extended care program; (4) the emergence of a variety of training programs, a research and evaluation department, and the beginnings of the Family Program. Accompanying this rehabilitative surge, the Literature Department, again encouraged by Butler, was giving signals that its own growth would soon be explosive.

Surveying the previous two decades, Pat Butler proudly wrote in 1970, "In 1949 Hazelden was founded through the spirit and courage of a few laymen. Without their leadership and that of their successors and friends, the lives of many individuals and their families might have been tragically different. Today the treatment center that was fashioned without a model is itself a model for other centers around the world." Hazelden represented Pat Butler's compassion for those in need.

*T*hanks to the generosity of Pat and Aimee Butler, Hazelden has had a corporate fine arts program for many years. Both of them, as well as others in the foundation, believed that Hazelden should never feel or look austere and institutional. They wanted it to seem instead like a home for those who came to receive treatment or other services—to be warm and inviting, and to demonstrate Hazelden's respect for the dignity of all. Because many patients not only feel down-and-out, but worthless, too, Pat and Aimee believed that displaying beautiful art in patient and public areas sends a positive message to patients.

In 1983, I began working with the Butlers and the corporate fine arts program. For a few years before the current art room was built, we met in what was actually a converted shower room/restroom in Butler Center. I always felt bad that we had two very fine and gracious individuals who had to have an art office in what had been a bathroom, but to Pat and Aimee, this was not a problem. Pat, in fact, didn't really want any office space at all.

—LORETTA ANDERSON

Chapter 10

HAZELDEN SINCE 1970

In the early seventies Butler seriously considered resigning as president of Hazelden. He was upset that Anderson was off campus so much and that both he and Gordon Grimm, a chaplain who developed and administered the training and educational programs for clergy, spent three weeks each June teaching at the Rutgers Summer School of Alcohol Studies. He felt that no one was home minding the store. He was also frustrated that he still had to balance the budget every year out of his own pockets. He was prevailed upon to stay, but he reorganized Hazelden in such a way that his concerns would be met.

any years ago, Pat Butler asked me to serve on the Hazelden Board of Trustees, and I did so for many years. Though I'd known Pat socially for many years, this was the first opportunity I'd had to see just how great his dedication to Hazelden was, and to learn of the tremendous contributions he'd made to the organization over the years.

In the late 1980s, Hazelden began a major capital-funds drive. Lou Hill, then chairman of the board, chose me to go to Florida to ask Pat for a contribution to the campaign. Though I knew Pat well, I was nevertheless a little nervous about this task, particularly when I learned how much they wanted me to ask him to contribute. I asked Lou, "Why me?!" But Lou replied, "Well, Bob, someone has to do it, and you know him as well as any of us, so it might as well be you."

I boarded a plane for Florida a few days later, and drove to Sanibel Island, a lovely place off the west coast of the state where Pat and Aimee were staying in their winter home. I called Pat and set up a lunch meeting. We chatted and got caught up on one another's lives.

Knowing I hadn't come all that way just to talk over lunch, Pat asked what he could do for me. I told him about the big capital-funds drive and explained what we planned to spend the money for. "I was sent to ask you for a contribution," I finally said, and he asked me how much I wanted.

I said, "Well, Pat, they told me to ask you for this amount," and then quickly added, "but if you think it's too much—"

Pat stopped me in midsentence, and then said, "No, that's not too much. Write me down for that amount."

In all the years I'd done fund-raising, both for Hazelden and for other organizations, I'd never had anyone else give me the first amount I'd asked for.

This was typical of Pat Butler. Not only was he a very generous person, but he was very dedicated to helping those who were having trouble with alcohol or other drugs. I believe Pat saw Hazelden as his legacy. He was determined to do what was right for the organization, and this contribution typified the level of commitment he had to it.

—BOB RIDDER

Harry Swift

Harry Swift, who joined Hazelden in 1966, served as president of the foundation 1986–1991. In Swift, Butler, who understood the importance of the bottom line, found a kindred spirit.

In a series of changes that gradually evolved between 1971 and 1975, Butler became the chairman of the board (1971), Anderson the president of Hazelden (1971), and Harry Swift the administrator (1975). A social worker, Swift had joined Hazelden in 1966 as a specialist in family problems relating to alcoholism. In the early seventies he developed the Hazelden Family Program. Butler's mandate to Swift was that he manage the budget (henceforward Hazelden was going to have to stand on its own two feet), pay attention to detail, and mind the store. The repositioning of Anderson allowed him to be off campus as much as he desired, spreading the Hazelden message. Butler readily appreciated Anderson's openness to new ideas. Both of them were visionaries. At the same time Butler was an astute businessman who understood the importance of the bottom line. Here he found a kindred soul in Swift.

Under Swift's administrative guidance from 1975 to 1985, Hazelden began breaking even for the first time in its history. Meanwhile, Butler and Anderson gave serious thought to the development and long-range planning of Hazelden's services. Pat Butler had been blessed with a comprehensive knowledge of the problems, needs, and potential solutions to the challenge of the disease of alcoholism. Wisdom and genius characterized his vision and activities on behalf of Hazelden. He possessed a natural instinct for perceiving the whole picture. He was continually suggesting or approving additions to Hazelden's continuum of care. In the seventies he encouraged Hazelden to develop educational materials and workshops to inform both patients and the public at large about substance abuse, early intervention, and prevention. His seminal vision of Hazelden's mission as being three-dimensional—(1) rehabilitation, (2) education and prevention, and (3) training for clergy, counselors, and other treatment professionals—fulfilled his personal and lifelong goal to provide the best help to the most alcoholics.

During the decade from 1975 to 1985 Hazelden experienced unprecedented growth. Educational Materials, Professional Services, and Training and Health Promotion began to forge their own identities at Hazelden alongside Rehabilitation Services. Prosperity, however, had a negative impact on the intimate spirit of smallness that had characterized Hazelden. Gradually, communication among the growing number of divisions within the organization began to break down. As the divisions became larger and more isolated from each other, they lost sight of the common purpose of all of them.

To help identify the problematic issues, in 1983 the Hazelden board requested that a management audit be performed. Butler reacted angrily when the audit, called the Byrd Report, suggested forming a two-tiered organizational structure that would once again place the financial running of Hazelden—as well as Human Resources, Marketing, Information Systems, and Research and Evaluation—in Anderson's hands. Butler did not believe that administration was Anderson's strength and felt it would be a mistake to return to pre-1975 days.

at was so very good at bringing a nucleus of people together when he wanted to have opinions on a new idea or project. But the real beauty of his skill was that people seldom realized that that's what he was doing. Pat was so very subtle in his groundwork. Looking back, perhaps this is why so many of his innovative ideas were successful—because all of them had been tried out on people—and the ones that didn't fly were just never stirred up much. In the best sense of the expression, Pat was a true political animal in that he always seemed to know exactly when to do what. And when he wanted to move on something, he knew how to make it happen.

—ELAINE WALKER

Moreover, Butler felt that the Byrd Report had dealt rather shabbily with Swift because it questioned his ability to serve as Hazelden's president upon the upcoming retirement of Anderson. The relationship between Butler and Swift had drifted into friendship over the years, and Butler never wavered in his support of Swift as Hazelden's president, despite the misgivings arising from the Byrd Report. After Swift's presidency ended in 1991, someone close to the scene commented that if Butler had remained in good health and alert of mind for the first decade of Swift's presidency then Swift may have lasted through those turbulent times. It is not surprising that a year after Butler's death, Swift was no longer president.

On the other hand, in later years Anderson and Butler drifted apart. While Butler's relationship with Swift was friendly and informal, with Anderson it was cordial but formal. Still, Butler and Anderson remained friendly with one another, respecting each other's talents and abilities and sharing as equal partners their vision for Hazelden. Butler would refer to Anderson as Hazelden's Hubert Humphrey because of his ability to communicate both on and off the cuff.

As the years passed, and his eighty-fifth birthday approached, Butler's body slowed down but his mind and desire for change and progress did not. Hazelden, which Butler himself described as his proudest accomplishment, continued to grow and expand with his encouragement. In 1984 Butler wrote a letter to all the members of Hazelden's board in which his customary perspicacity, foresight, and wisdom were readily apparent. In referring to the growth of Hazelden over the past thirty-five years, he noted that the scope of activities had gone far beyond what the founding fathers of Hazelden could ever have imagined. He believed that they would have been aghast at the range of activities that Hazelden was presently engaged in, and doing them all in such a competent fashion. In looking to the future, Hazelden would have to explore additional opportunities to be of service to people.

Butler felt that Hazelden should be willing to discuss and explore the applicability of its technology to the treatment of other addictions, observing that some people in recovery literally kill themselves with food and tobacco addictions. Were Hazelden to enter into these other fields he believed that its staff was quite capable of constructing an appropriate peer group model for them. Quite poignantly he inquired in a letter, "Should the 'pioneer' be lagging behind the competition?" He strongly believed that Hazelden should consider the potential application of the Twelve Steps and the self-help model to other chronic illnesses. "In summary," he wrote, "I think we should keep our options open—all of them."

*A*nother major debate occurred over whether Hazelden should treat people who were addicted to drugs besides alcohol—heroin, cocaine, and so on. We'd traditionally treated only alcoholics, but other drugs were becoming a huge national problem, particularly among our young people. There were alumni, however, who didn't want any "long-haired hippies" at Hazelden. Yet at the same time, we were getting calls from alumni whose own children were having trouble with these drugs. They wanted to send their kids to Hazelden for help. Despite the trauma and controversy, Pat was always able to stay calm. Over and over, he said, "We simply have to help these people. We can't turn our backs on them." And we didn't.

—HARRY SWIFT

BUTLER'S FORMULA FOR SUCCESS AT HAZELDEN

As Hazelden grew, Butler's dedication and discipline allowed him to initiate the delicate balance between structure and spirit and to select leaders both astute and prudent enough to maintain that balance. He had an unfailing instinct for the particular and the pragmatic that was essential for Hazelden's survival. At each critical stage of Hazelden's development Butler was able to evoke Hazelden's potential for growth, not simply in terms of new buildings, but also in terms of vigorous service.

Because he personally brought patients to Center City, Butler knew how well staff did their jobs, from admissions to aftercare, and he was always suggesting ways to provide better care and service. When his suggestions did not receive the immediate attention he thought they deserved, he would regularly remind those responsible of his expectations. There was a certain set of his jaw that signified when Butler was not happy with things. He was persistent and liked to have loose ends tied up as quickly as possible. It was not a rare occasion when he let Anderson, or Swift, or Grimm know when something was not getting done.

But amid the focus on institutions and programs, mission and vision, one must not lose sight of Pat Butler's warm, caring, and personal style. In the early years of Hazelden, when the board of directors held its quarterly meetings at Fellowship Club, Butler would send a handwritten thank-you note to staff speaking to their graciousness and hard work in accommodating the board. He took time to talk with patients and staff and to send unexpected notes or postcards to staff members celebrating some event or remembering a good work that the staff member had done. Always the gentleman, thankful and considerate, he made everyone feel important. He would visit their offices and elicit their ideas and suggestions to improve patient services. Traveling to Center City and Fellowship Club and conversing with staff and patients were among his happiest moments.

*D*uring my early years at Hazelden, in the late 1970s and early 1980s, I knew Pat through my work as a counselor, supervisor, and eventually as director of Pioneer House— what we now call the Hazelden Center for Youth and Families.

Pat was always very in tune with what was happening in terms of Hazelden's services and staff in Center City; it was uncanny, really, considering that he didn't spend that much time on campus.

Here's an example. Since I spent most of my time at Pioneer House, I saw Pat, at most, once every couple months. I didn't think he really even knew who I was. At one of the first lunches I attended after a board of trustees meeting, however, Pat turned to me and said, "I understand that your sister's getting married this weekend." I was completely *shocked* that he knew this, and to this day, I haven't a clue as to where he got that information!

As I got to know him better, I realized that Pat did know me, and that he knew all the Hazelden staff. He had a wonderful way of getting to know people through casual conversation in hallways, in the dining room— wherever he could—and he simply paid attention to what people said. He cared about us, he really listened, and he remembered what we said.

Pat was very committed to the clients we had at Pioneer House. I always respected him for that because at that time, at least, it was my impression that, frankly, a lot of the older people in the recovery community tended to be rather unconnected to the younger generation.

But not Pat. Each quarter, advisory board meetings were held at Pioneer House, and Pat always attended them. Working with adolescents and young adults, we learned that we had to prepare food that they'd want to eat—and that meant meals like mashed potatoes, gravy, canned peas, and a pork chop weren't on the menu! After one of these meetings while Pat and I were eating *lunch in the dining room, it suddenly occurred to me that I was sitting next to a guy in his late 70s who had no doubt eaten in some of the finest restaurants in the world. But here we were in the middle of all these kids eating tacos and corn dogs. I felt concerned and began to apologize for the food, but Pat stopped me and said, "No, no, Mike, don't worry about it. Everything's fine."*

I was so struck by this. There wasn't an ounce of nonacceptance in the man, and here was another example that just said it all.

—Mike Schiks

One morning, nearly ten years ago now, while I was working as the director of Residential Programs in Center City, I found a postcard in my mail postmarked from Florida. On the front was an image of three pelicans sitting on a pier. I was a bit puzzled because I couldn't imagine who'd be sending me such a postcard.

When I turned it over, I saw that it was from Pat Butler. The note on the back said, "I don't know why, but these pelicans reminded me of you, Damian. So I just thought I'd send you this card."

This kind of action was so typical of Pat. He would do these touching and thoughtful little things for people just on a whim. In this case, a card with some pelicans would probably not have meant much, if anything, to someone else, but to me, at that time, it really meant a lot. At that point in my life, it was rather important.

Again, it just typified the thoughtfulness of this man. Here he's on vacation in Florida, getting on in years, and just happened to think about me when he saw that card in a store. In and of itself, this isn't so unusual; we're often reminded of people we know in the course of our daily lives. But Pat took this a step further by taking the time to buy the card, jot down a short note, and send it to me. Well, I was very moved by this. As I look back, while he did many other things like this, this particular gesture really stands out for me.

—DAMIAN MCELRATH

Chapter 11

FINAL YEARS

As Butler approached his ninetieth birthday, his health began to fail. After a stroke that slowed him down considerably, he stepped down as chairman of Hazelden's board but remained an active board member until his death. He was extremely upset by his family's decision that he should no longer drive. His daybooks reveal that he continued to exercise daily, that he visited Center City and Fellowship Club weekly, that he went to AA meetings regularly, that he liked to listen to the Twins and Vikings games on radio, that he went to the St. Paul Athletic Club several times a week, and that he liked to read and play solitaire. Aimee, who had to have two shifts of nurses during the day for herself, was his loving and best companion and friend. Their apartment at 740 Riverside Drive was adorned with Aimee's art collection, the trophies and ribbons won by their horses, and Pat and Aimee's extensive library, which demonstrated an eclectic taste, the most recent editions being on religious philosophy and history.

Aimee and Pat were very affectionate and deferential to one another. Aimee never nagged him and during the day had her own

Pat and Aimee Butler in their later years

things to do. Pat was an early riser and after his meditation and quiet time would make breakfast for Aimee. They never complained of their pains and were very considerate of one another. In 1990 they celebrated sixty-four years of married life and during all of that time Aimee continued to choose her husband's daily ties. Both enjoyed reading and the quiet time that they had with one another. A member of the Audubon Society, Pat enjoyed birdwatching. Aimee liked to shop and read. She was a lover of art, and her artist friends were her constant companions.

The concern that Pat had for his wife's health in the earlier years of their marriage was greatly relieved by her gradual recovery as she developed interests beyond home life. She adopted Pat's interest in thoroughbred jumping horses, traveling with him and sharing his enjoyment. In addition, and probably of most importance, she was particularly pleased to be involved in the new buildings at Hazelden. In a sense, from that point forward, Hazelden became a family affair for Aimee as well as for Pat. She began to complement Pat's vision for Hazelden with her own genius, affirming and promoting Hazelden's emphasis on the singular dignity of each individual who entered there. Over the years, her instincts for color, light, art, nature, and architectural imagery and symmetry resulted in enhancing Hazelden's environment to the enrichment of the patient's dignity.

We Americans often make a lot of the differences between generations in this culture, but Pat was a guy who easily transcended them. He and I were able to connect on all levels, not just about experiences that were connected to addiction and recovery. I could talk about anything with him, including girlfriend problems, work hassles, just whatever. And it wasn't like he took a problem-solving approach—he was just so empathic. He was able to help me laugh about my troubles and problems, and then we'd laugh about them together. He was just such an easy person to talk with—truly warm and genuine. We might just as well have been peers—actually, we were peers. We had a wonderful rapport. He was so positive, so enthusiastic about life—and about associating with me.

Over time, Pat and Aimee began to invite me over to their house on Friday evenings. Then, after dinner together, I'd drive them to Friday night meetings at Fellowship Club. Our friendship continued like this until about 1990, when Pat became seriously ill.

I realized then, and still can say today, that it was one of the greatest privileges of my life to know Pat.

—MARK ROSE